The Way of Hope

by C. Alan Ames

1st printing, August 1997 — 20,000 copies

Printed and Distributed in the U.S.A. by:

The 101 Foundation, Inc.
P.O. Box 151
Asbury, New Jersey 08802-0151

Phone: 908-689 8792
Fax: 908-689 1957

Dedication

For my mother, who bore much from me in my youth,
and my brothers Sean, Dermot, Herbert, and Dennis,
and their families.
With grateful thanks to all those who have helped
me throughout the world, especially
Mr. and Mrs. Tom and Anne Rochfort, and my editors.

Books Available from the 101 Foundation in the U.S., and also from the following:

New Zealand
Patrick J. Clegg
P. O. Box 31495
Lower Hutt
New Zealand
Phone & Fax: 644 566 5786

Ireland
Touch of Heaven
66 Landscape Park
Churchtown
Dublin 14, Ireland
Phone & Fax: 01-298 5403

England
Angelus Communications
22 Milbury Drive
Littleborough
Lancashire OL15 OBZ
England
Phone & Fax: 01706 372 674

Australia
Touch of Heaven
P. O. Box 85
Wembley
Western Australia 6014
Phone 09-275 6608
Fax: 619-382 4392

ISBN # 1-890137-06-5

Carver Alan Ames was born in England in 1953. His childhood and adulthood were turbulent. He married Kathryn and moved to Australia and raised two children. Then in 1993, angels, saints, and the Holy Trinity began communicating with him.

At that time, he experienced a mini-judgment, and fell totally in love with Jesus. From a violent man, he has become child-like with a complete devotion to God. Alan and his wife left their jobs in August of 1996 to devote their time fully to do God's work, founding the Touch of Heaven ministry.

Preface

by C. Alan Ames
July 17, 1997

The Lord God, Jesus Christ, has been speaking and appearing to me in visions since February, 1994. At first I did not write anything down, but later I was asked by God to take up a pen and record what I was experiencing. I began to recieve receive daily messages from the Trinity, angels, and the saints, some of which are in this book, *The Way Of Hope.*

On the sixth of February, 1996, Jesus started to show me some episodes of His life on earth. Through His eyes, I began to see singular incidents that took place as He traveled with His disciples through the towns and villages in the Holy Land. While this was happening, He also granted me the grace to perceive His thoughts.

As I saw and heard these scenes of God's love before me, I was often overwhelmed with tears of sadness or joy. It seemed that at each revelation there was a lesson to be learned and pondered upon, for by revealing these events He was teaching us how to live and to love.

In Judas, I began to see all the weaknesses that so many of us have and, when we ignore or forget God, who is always with us and ready to help us, how easy it is to be lead away from Him. In Judas, I was also shown that the Lord Jesus will forgive any mistakes we make in life, because He loves us so much. All we need to do is to accept His love and to ask for His forgiveness. The temptations, feelings, problems, and desires of men at that time were much the same as those of today.

Perhaps one reason that the Lord is giving these insights is to show us that it is possible to conquer self and to conquer sin. We need only to call upon God, as His help is never failing. "Ask and thou shalt receive." In these passages, He shows us the way.

The visions and words continue.

Table of Contents

The Way of Hope

to C. Alan Ames

*C*hapter *l.*

What Lies Ahead...

Lord Jesus—12/22/95

...Either Heaven

There is a glorious gift awaiting all, a gift of love, a gift of eternal life, of eternal joy. Isn't it a wonderful thought that, after this life, there is a place where you can rest in joyful peace and love, a place where you are happy, where there is no need, no poverty, no anger, no hate...nothing but love.

Wouldn't you think with this, an offer to all, that every man, woman, and child would spend their lives on earth trying to reach this paradise? It is not that mankind does not know of its existence, for mankind has been told from the beginning of its creation. Mankind has been told over and over what a glorious reward there is for living a good life in the love of God.

As a child, if your parents said to you, "If you behave well, on the weekend we will take you to the fair," some would find it hard to be good all week, but their loving parents would make allowances for this, and the little wrongs they did would be forgiven. It would only be serious problems that would stop the parents from rewarding their children.

Then, at the end of the week, together the children and the parents would enjoy the time at the fair. The parents not only participating with the children, but also just watching their children having fun. This is the true love that can be found in family, the love of each other, and the love of being united with your family.

...Or Purgatory

It is the same with the Father in Heaven. He says to His children, "Lead a good life and receive the rewards of Heaven." The Father knows many will struggle, many will make mistakes, but the Father will forgive them if they truly seek forgiveness. It is only when the children continue to sin, ignore God's love, and treat each other with contempt, that the Father may delay the giving of their life in Heaven.

Because the Father loves us so much, He does not wish to deny anyone the joy of eternal life in Heaven, so in His mercy, He places those who have made mistakes into Purgatory where they can atone for their sins, and where they can come to understand what God's love truly is. Once they do this, then the Father welcomes them into Heaven with open arms and a full heart, full of love, to share with them. When they are in Heaven, together with the Father, they share the joy of each other's love, and the Father is happy just to sit and watch them in their new life of love.

...Or Hell

Sometimes people do not stop sinning, do not start loving, and slip deeper and deeper into evil. The Father is so sad when this happens, for He does not want to lose one child, so the Father offers, over and over, help to guide these children back to His love. Still some of these children refuse God's help to guide them, and in their acceptance of evil, they start to hate God. With all this hate and anger, they try to hurt those who do love God. They try to take God's children to where they are, and this is immersed in evil. Over and over, God offers them His help, His love, His heart, and over and over, some still reject it.

The Father then allows these lost ones what they seek. He gives them the rewards they long for. It is only when they are completely lost, completely in evil, that the Father opens the doors to Hell for them. The Father cries from His heart every time the doors are opened and another soul is lost. The Father, like any parent of love, only wants to see His children happy. How sad it is when one is lost.

When the doors of Hell close behind a lost soul, they then see to what they have committed themselves for eternity. It is then they beg for mercy, a mercy that was always there for them, but which they denied. The evil one is there in his hatred, in his anger, and in his fury. Then they find the rewards of sin, the rewards of living away from God. Then they find no mercy, only pain; no love, only hate; no joy, only misery. They are swamped in a sea of fire, a fire that burns and burns, a fire that never ends, a fire that endures forever.

Describing what lies ahead for many when they take the next step which leads to life eternal, will fill most with awe, with wonder, with joy. Others will be filled with disbelief, will reject what they read, will say it is ridiculous...it cannot be true. It is the truth, whether or not people believe it, Heaven, Purgatory and Hell do exist. They are the truths of life. It is this life on earth that is only a pathway to your true eternal life. It is the choices you make now that lead you to your true existence, an existence of love or an existence of suffering.

In the descriptions that follow, I will show you what awaits those who come to Heaven, go to Purgatory, or descend into Hell. Because I love you all, I will tell you the truth, so that you can be clear in what choices you make and in what the rewards are. It may shock some, sicken some, but it needs to be told to awaken those who do not believe.

To start, to those who do not consider what lies ahead or think about their future, always remember the choices are mankind's and the rewards you receive are those you sought. If you remember that your God's mercy is there for all who want it, for all who seek it, then know all can be saved, all can avoid the suffering and pain of Hell, all can come to Heaven and share in the love of God. My Father, My Holy Spirit, and I, your friend, Jesus Christ, long for all mankind to accept Our love and become saints in Heaven.

Heaven

What a glorious place, full of love, full of peace, full of enjoyment. Think of the happiest moment in your life, and then magnify that a billion times, and it does not compare to the smallest of touches of Heaven. When you are in Heaven, you are so full of God's love, you know nothing else except complete ecstasy, an ecstasy which increases and increases.

Each soul in Heaven is a mirror of God's love, and so when you see each other, you see God's love and are lifted in ecstasy even more. Just when you think you have all the joy you could ever desire, the Father fills you with more and more; you become a light burning brighter and brighter in God's love. You come to understand this will never end, it will only increase as the Father has an unlimited supply of love to share. As you enter each doorway in Heaven, you find wonders and joys you could never have imagined. You find everyone in love with you and you in love with them, you soar in unison with them in singing the praises of God and, as you do, you are filled with even more love from the Father.

All the saints you have heard of are there and you see the pure beauty of their love. You see the angels and archangels and together you fly throughout eternity looking upon all the wonders God has made. You come to understand the joy of God in everything He has created. You see beautiful valleys filled with the most fragrant flowers, you see spirits of love waiting to play with you, waiting to share their love with you. You see mountains of golden light exploding into a cascade of light that touches you and fills you with joy. You see rivers of so many beautiful colors, all flowing to join as a sea of wonderful fountains, that when you bathe in them your whole being resounds with happiness.

You see all around you lovely delicacies, and when you taste them you are engulfed in the warmth of love. As you take the hands of your companion saints in Heaven and look to the Father, your spirit explodes like a firework in joyful love. As the light from your spirit is touched by those around you, every spirit unites to become one with God and then you feel what you never thought possible. You feel all the love in eternity entering into you...you feel and see all the good things that have happened...you become part of all these things... you become part of all the love that has been shared among mankind, among the angels, among the saints... you become part of every moment of love that has ever happened. Then you understand what Heaven truly is.

Purgatory

Many people do not believe in Purgatory. They say yes to Heaven, yes to Hell, but no to Purgatory. Purgatory does exist, it is real and many do go there. Purgatory should not be thought of as a place where you suffer and suffer, but more as a place where you repent for your sins, and a place where your spirit is purified so that you may enter Heaven. If a spirit is unclean, then it is impossible for it to enter Heaven, no matter how small the sin may be. This is what Purgatory is for, to cleanse the spirit of its sins.

When a soul enters Purgatory it enters with the knowledge of how it has offended God. This knowledge by itself is enough to make the soul sink into anguish for its wrongs, the soul knows the pain of offending God and is filled with shame, with sorrow, with regret.

Then, through the darkness of such an experience, shines a light, so warm, so loving, coming closer and closer, and then before you is your Lord who embraces you and says to you, "You have made amends, your spirit is clean, you are welcome in Heaven." Your Lord takes your hand and leads you to eternal love in Heaven, a love that was always there for you, it was only that you denied it.

Hell

Hell is a place where none should go, a place that should be empty of God's children, a place that should not receive one soul. Hell is there for those who sink completely into sin, for whom there is no hope, who are an abomination to God's love. Hell is full of pain, of anguish, of torment, of suffering. Hell is a place to be avoided, a place of never ending suffering which increases and increases.

Understand what hell is now and reject it, for I love you all and I want none to go there. Now you have been told of the glory of Heaven, the sadness of Purgatory and the terror of Hell. Now believe, reassess how you live your life, see what can be yours if you decide to follow God's commands and live in God's love.

See also what awaits if you turn your back on God. See the suffering you will endure forever. I ask you to think deeply now and make the right choice, the choice for God.

I know many will not believe, many will say if there is a God, He is a God of love who will forgive us no matter what we do. Well, this is true, but God will only forgive you if you repent. Any suffering you face is brought upon you by your own free will, not by God. Understand that you make this choice, and you make the payment if you choose evil.

Some of you will say that after death there is nothing. Well, if that is so, you have nothing to fear, but know this; there is eternal life and your denying it will not stop the payment you will have to make when you die.

I want you all to understand clearly what awaits you so that you will make the correct choice and you will be happy forever. Do not close your eyes to reality, do not close your hearts to love, and do not lose your souls to evil.

†††

7.

Lord Jesus—10/23/95

My Love

Into your hearts I ask you to place My love, for when it is within you there is only one destiny that awaits you, the destiny of love. If you can live your lives with God's love as the center of your existence then there is only gladness and joy at the end of this life.

In your lives ahead, surround yourselves and your families and friends with My love, and fear nothing. Once you are in My love, there is nothing that you should be frightened of, there is nothing that can harm you, for I protect you. It may be that in this life you have difficult times, but if you can overcome them in My love, the rewards are great.

You will have nothing to fear for you will be brought to Heaven in glory, you will be welcomed into Heaven by God's love, and you will know all your hard times, all your difficult moments, were but a stepping stone to the greatest reward of all, eternal life with God. Throughout your lives, if you hold firm to My love, the love of Jesus, then all the trials, all the moments of despair, all the times of temptation will be easier to overcome.

Today there are many prophecies of the times that lie ahead. Many tell of what is to come, many speak of the evil one's child coming to destroy mankind. These are the messages I give to warn mankind what will happen if it does not change. The most important aspect of these messages is often ignored and only the spectacular, the frightening, the disasters are considered. The most important part of the messages is that if mankind changes and comes back to God's love in prayer, penance, and the sacraments, then all the difficulties can be avoided. Prayer and love of God will always defeat evil and if they are embraced by all mankind, then evil cannot take hold of My children and hurt them.

Remember, evil can only flourish where it is accepted; deny it in love and prayer, then see evil disappear from the planet. Mankind has always had a free choice and it still has; if mankind makes the choice of God now, then there is nothing to fear in the future. Deny God and there is so much to fear, so much to be concerned over. Make the right choice now and be spared the pain you may bring upon yourselves.

(The Lord now asked me to read Leviticus 26: God's promises to them that keep His commandments and the punishments with which He threatens transgressions.)

Lord Jesus—10/30/95

Warnings To Prevent Disasters

With every moment that passes on earth a spirit can be saved or a spirit can be lost. What happens today is that so many are lost, more and more each day. When the world is told what is happening it turns its back upon the truth and prefers to listen to and believe lies. There are so many warnings given in recent times, so many pleas to return to God's love, but most people ignore them, discard them, and carry on living as though nothing has been said.

Look at the warnings and the signs that were given at Fatima. See what God did through His handmaiden, My Mother Mary. The sun danced, the skies changed, and those who were there believed...but how many others did? How many look at the messages given and see that they have come to be?

When the Church listened to My Mother's word, Russia was saved. It may have taken some time, but it happened. It is the same with all the messages given; they will happen but it may not be in the time scale that man expects. Prayers can delay or even prevent disasters happening, so if messages of destruction or evil happenings are given, they are given to encourage the people to pray, to change, and in this way they can prevent them occurring.

†††

Lord Jesus—11/13/95

Messages Same As Holy Scripture

Mankind needs to listen and understand what has been said in Holy Scripture, then look and see that the messages given in recent times are the same; the words may be different but the messages are the same. Repent and pray, love and hope, trust and help.

Repent and pray so that the world changes and returns to God's love. Love God, and hope that in God's mercy all will seek forgiveness. Trust God, and help each other to find the true path to Heaven.

When mankind looks to Holy Scripture, he will find the same messages throughout; when mankind listens to My Mother's messages, he will find the same messages throughout; when mankind listens to My true prophets, he will find the same messages throughout.

The messages never change, it is only mankind's understanding of them that does. Mankind must start to listen to what his Creator says to him. The Creator, the Father, does not keep sending messages without a reason, He sends them because He loves all of mankind and does not want to lose one soul. He sends them because His love and His forgiveness are unlimited, and He will never deny them to any of His children who truly ask. He sends them because He wants each heart, each soul, each spirit in Heaven with Him to share in His eternal joy and happiness.

The Father looks upon His children and despairs to see so many refuse to listen to His advice, His help, His love. All the Father ever asks is for goodness, for caring, for sharing. All the Father ever asks for is love. Why is it so difficult to listen and understand these words? Why is it so easy to ignore them?

Parents should look to their children and see how they give their children good advice which is only meant to help, to encourage, and to guide safely through life. Then see how often the children ignore this advice, sometimes with disastrous results. It is then that the parents say if only they had listened, if only they had changed, if only they were more careful. The parents in the world should see that the Father offers them the same advice, and that if they ignore it, the results could be disastrous for them. Children should look and see how many times their parents' advice was right, was for their best interest, and then see the Father in Heaven giving them good advice, and listen to it. The family of mankind is the Father's family for He created it, and as a Father, He sends over and over His advice, His helping hand, His directions so as to avoid disasters. He does this because the Father loves His family on earth. Now, mankind, listen and show the Father you love Him.

†††

Chapter 2.

Seeking God's Help To Do His Will

Lord Jesus—12/23/95

The Error In Relying On One's Self

Mankind in itself cannot find what it seeks. Mankind is always looking for answers but never finds them; it doesn't find them because it looks in the wrong places and for the wrong reasons. If the children of God can come to accept that looking for answers within themselves and only relying on themselves to find the answers can only lead to wrong answers, if then they accept that it is only with God's help that all they seek can be found and ask for God's help, they will see all is possible and all can be answered truthfully.

God, in His mercy, made His children in His own image and gave them the abilities to be loving guardians of His paradise, His garden of Eden. With this comes the responsibilities of caring for and sharing with all of the other creations of God that are placed in mankind's care. This is a special gift God gives to all His children to show the depth of His love.

God is saying to His children, "I created all this, and now I give it to you to watch over and protect in love." Imagine then, how God must feel when He sees the special gift being destroyed and treated with contempt. Imagine how God feels each time a species He has created is destroyed, the planet He has created being used as a thing that is only there for man's needs and man's pleasure. With the giving of this gift, this trust, God asked mankind to look after all things, not to exploit them.

God gave mankind a perfect creation designed to be self-renewing, self-sufficient, and self-supporting. This creation was also given as a gift through which mankind could develop, develop in love, together with God's helping hand. As mankind developed, it should have been with consideration for the total gift being given, not just for itself. It is in this way that mankind could show its thanks and respect for its Creator. With progress, the children of God should have come closer to God and should have seen the beauty and wonder in all of God's creations and treasured them.

What has happened in mankind's development is that often people have only considered themselves, and in most cases ignored all else. It seems that men think they can treat the planet, the air, the animals how they like, regardless of the results. Each time men and women destroy a species or wreck the environment, they detract from God's gift to them. Each time they destroy, mankind does not see that a creation of God is taken from the total environment that was given to them.

Man does not see that God created each thing for a reason, even if man cannot understand the reason. God created each thing to perform a role in the self-sufficient gift God gave to mankind. To remove anything from its role starts to change the design God had for mankind and this earth. It starts to unlock all that God had placed in man's care. Then, as time goes on, more and more are destroyed and so the creation of God becomes changed, becomes something other than what it was meant to be. It becomes a living hell for many and eventually an agony for all.

Lord Jesus—12/26/95

Live In Love

A great future can be mankind's if it is prepared to change and live in love, not out of it. To live in love means to love God, to love each other, and to love and respect what God has given you to care for. If, united in love, the world opens its heart to God and listens to God's will and responds in love, then the earth can once again become the paradise it was created to be. Each person's heart can also become the gift of love that it is created to be and each moment can become the joy it was given to be. Mankind can make the changes required, the changes of heart; it only has to try to, then God, through His only true Son Jesus, will offer His helping hand to guide mankind home.

The offer has always been there, but usually men's ears are closed. Open them now and accept the offer of God's love and find the true peace and joy that is mankind's inheritance as children of God.

Lord Jesus—12/30/95

Sin Covers The World With Darkness

The pain that all the lonely, all the lost, all the abused, all the tortured children of God carry in their hearts weighs heavy on the scales of justice. Can not mankind see that sin accumulates and grows; as it grows it covers the world with it's darkness. Even those who love God find it hard to overcome. It seems the more you love God the heavier the load.

As the world is covered, so it chokes, so it struggles to survive. Evil now attacks everything on the earth be it the smallest of God's creations or the largest. Evil is gnawing away at God's creations of love and is doing so by the blindness and ignorance of mankind. Eventually it will reach a point where man will have to open his eyes and remove the cloud from his mind. It may be too late by then for the damage will have already been done and the remedy will be hard. It is better to treat this sickness now before it has taken almost total hold. If you do this, the treatment required will be much easier to accept.

All that is needed is to accept the Holy Trinity as the one true God, to offer God your love in prayer and the sacraments, and to live God's commandments. So little is asked for now, but it seems so much; if, however, it is ignored, then in the future much more will be needed and mankind will wonder why it didn't give the little before.

Lord Jesus—1/14/96

Respond In Kindness

If a person were to look upon another who was sick, struggling to survive, and reaching the end of his resources, surely most people would want to help if it was within their means to do so. Most people would offer some assistance, some help, even if it meant they had to sacrifice a little. Most people would open their hearts to the one in need and show kindness; it would only be the cold of heart that would refuse.

Today the world is sick, is struggling to survive and is reaching the end of it's resources. The people today need to respond in kindness...kindness to those in need... kindness to those who are sick, starving, oppressed... kindness to the planet which has been abused for so long...kindness to the animals which have been exploited for so long.

Now is the time for mankind to unite as a family and to offer help to each other, to offer love to each other, and with each other, work towards renewing the planet that is God's gift to mankind. If the people close their hearts and remain indifferent or uncaring to what is happening on the earth, then they allow the evil one to destroy God's gift to mankind even more. By their action they open their arms to welcome evil into their lives, lives which will only be rewarded with suffering and pain.

Now mankind needs to become aware that its future is in its own hands; mankind has free choice of good or evil. Make the wrong choice and regret it in eternity. Make the right choice, the choice of God, the choice which means to help to share, to unite in love as one family, and then enjoy eternal life with God.

15.

Accept God's Will

In life, finding the right path to walk is not easy; every moment is a choice, a choice of accepting God's will in your life or denying it. It is with these choices that you decide your future, the future of your family on earth, your planet's future and your soul's future. It is with these choices that comes the responsibility of guiding others along the same path as you, for others, who see how you live and act, often imitate your actions.

With so much at stake with each choice it is important that the correct ones are made and this can only happen if you ask for God's help. If you try to make these choices without God, then you are assured to make the wrong ones which will only destroy all you love. The choices are choices of life or death; choose wisely with God's help and be rewarded with eternal peace.

††††

Chapter 3.

How To Live

Lord Jesus—6/17/95

To help a friend is a special gift, but to help a stranger
 is a grace.
To help a person you know is not difficult, but to
 help an unknown person is harder.
To help someone you love is easy, but to help someone
 you are unattached to is at times difficult.
Always show your love of God by helping all who ask,
 by showing your love to strangers, and by bringing
 yourself to those in need of help.

Sleeping with God brings peace and comfort.
Sleeping with God brings joy.
Sleeping with God brings love.
When you sleep with God, your spirit is renewed.
When you sleep with God, your spirit is strengthened,
And when you sleep with God, your spirit is joined
 in love with God.

God the Father—6/18/95

The love I have for you, I have for all.
The love I give you, I give all.
The love I offer you, I offer all.
I have enough love for all and I offer it to all freely.
I want only to give My love, but all need to accept
 it to receive it.

Corpus Christi, a special day and a special gift.
The body of God for man.

Full of love, full of joy, full of Jesus when you receive
the Eucharist.

Full of truth, full of light, full of God when you receive
the bread of life.

Full of sweetness, full of beauty, full of the Spirit when
you receive the body of Jesus.

Eat of the body within the bread and become one
celebration with God in the Eucharist.

Lord Jesus—6/18/95

Bread and wine, body and blood.
Bread and wine, fruit of love.
Bread and wine, Jesus the Lord.

God the Father—6/19/95

For those in love with God, your love is My treasure,
your love is My joy, your love is My gift I first
gave to you, and now you return it to Me.

Your faith is a wonderful painting of love made up
of each stroke of pain that you overcame in My
love.

Your faith is a glorious sunrise that sets each day
alight in truth.

Your faith is oh, so special to Me, that each moment
I look upon it and enjoy the love that radiates from
it.

Old friends, new friends, and true friends...everyone
should be treated as an old friend and everyone
should be treated as a new friend; this is how you
become a true friend of all.

Lord Jesus—6/19/95

When you see those I have chosen, praise them.
When you hear those I have chosen, listen to them
and,

When you meet those I have chosen, encourage them.
There are many I have chosen and, like you, they
need support and help.

When I give to you, I give in love.
When I offer, I offer love.
When I speak, I speak of love.
When you receive, receive in love.
When you accept, accept for love.
When you use, use because of love.
Offering and giving show true love.
Receiving and giving show true faith.

Doubting, disbelieving, not trusting, these are what stop
My love healing My children.
Accepting, believing, and trusting, these are what open
My children to My healing love.
Tell them just to accept, trust, and believe and all
is there for them.

St. Peter—6/21/95

Rome was the end of my life, but the beginning of
eternity with God.
Rome was the end of my path to Jesus Christ and
the beginning of my eternal rest in Heaven.
Rome was where I showed how much I loved Jesus
Christ, true God and true man, when I gave my
life for Him.

Lord Jesus—6/21/95

Blood of love, gift to God.
Blood of love, gift from the Savior.
Blood of love, gift to the Savior.

19.

God   the   Father—6/22/95

My Son looks upon the world and His heart breaks for those who turn their backs on God. Sweet Jesus cries from His soul for those who, by their stupidity, destroy themselves. The heart of Jesus bleeds and bleeds with a river of love and forgiveness flowing from it. He offers His love, His friendship, and His hope to all; if only all would accept it, happiness would reign supreme. Accept what is offered and accept the truth of eternity.

The truth never changes, it is only man's interpretation of it that does.

God   the   Father—6/22/95

A lone figure hangs on the cross,
A lone heart gives itself to God,
A lone spirit unites with God.
On the cross My Son Jesus hung alone, opening His heart to His children and united with the Spirit in God.
The children only need to accept Jesus' heart into theirs to receive the Spirit and be united with God.

God   the   Father—6/23/95

Sweet heart of Jesus,
Sacred heart of Jesus,
Holy heart of Jesus,
Open heart of Jesus,
True heart of Jesus,
True heart of God,
Heart of Jesus.

A day of love, the day of Jesus' heart,
A day of giving and receiving, the day of Jesus' heart.
A day of God's grace, the day of Jesus' heart.

Oh   sacred   heart,
Oh   heart   divine,
Oh   heart   forever   thine.

Oh   sacred   heart,
Oh   heart   so   sweet,
Oh   heart   that   evil   did   not   defeat.

Oh   sacred   heart,
Oh   heart   of   love,
Oh   heart   of   God,   a   gift   from   above.

Lord   Jesus—6/23/95

My   heart   bleeds   with   droplets   of   love.
My   heart   weeps   with   tears   of   blood.
My   heart   opens   with   floods   of   mercy.
My   merciful   heart   opens   to   show   the   love   of   God   and
My   sacred   heart   opens   to   flood   the   world   with   My
   love.

*Vision,   before   Mass,   of   millions   of   nuns   and   priests
carrying   crosses   behind   Jesus.   Many   were   throwing   their
crosses   away   and   leaving,   and   so   those   who   remained,
their   crosses   got   larger   and   heavier.*

Lord   Jesus—6/24/95

Under   the   cross   stands   a   redeeming   grace   for   all   those
   who   want   it.
Under   the   cross   stands   a   redeeming   way   for   all   those
   who   follow   it.
Under   the   cross   stands   a   redeeming   gift   for   all   those
   who   will   accept   it.
It   is   the   gift   of   My   gracious   Mother,   who   shows   the
   way   to   her   Son.

Our Lady—6/24/95

A friend, a companion, a love, Jesus.
A brother, a father, a loved one, Jesus.
God, redeeming Savior, love, Jesus.

Lord Jesus—6/24/95

Bring your love to Me, and in return receive Mine.
Bring yourself to Me, and in return receive Me.
Bring your heart to Me, and in return receive love.
Love is Mine to give, for I am love.
Love is yours to receive, for I offer it.
Love is there to fill you, for I pour it out on you.
Whatever you do, do it in love.
Whatever you do, do it for love.
Whatever you do, do for Me, for I am love.

Around your heart, place My love,
Around your soul, place My blood,
Around your spirit, place My grace,
And be strong in Me.

Feeding souls is the only true food to give,
Feeding souls is the only true way to live,
Feeding souls is the only true salvation,
Feeding souls is the only way to build a nation,
Feeding souls is the only way to Heaven,
Feeding souls is the only way to save your brethren.

Full of love, full of joy, full of hope;
When you are full of these you are full of God.

Lord Jesus—6/27/95 (after Communion)

My body, a gift, My love, a grace.
My life, a living gift, gracefully brought to earth through
  Mary, My Mother.

One Man, one love, one God.
One Spirit, one light, one God.
One Father, one Creator, one God.
God in Spirit, in Man, in the Creator.
A divine mystery, a divine love, a divine truth.

Along the path to Heaven you will find many tired, falling, struggling souls. Bring a renewed strength to them, offer a helping hand to them, and show them the right path.

Lord Jesus—6/28/95 (about the Pope)

A son who is a father,
A father who is a servant,
A servant who is a saint.

God the Father—6/29/95

Riding the crest of the wave can only last until the wave breaks; then the next wave arrives and you are carried to its crest. So it is in life with God; you will ride many waves, but also you will find many breaks. You will find, however, as each wave gets larger so each break gets harder.

God the Father—6/29/95 (for Monastery meeting)

Oh My dear little ones, to look to your brethren and only see with eyes of love, is what My Son Jesus taught.
To look to your brethren and see what you can do for them, not what they can do for you, is what My Son Jesus taught.
To look to your brethren as your family united in God, is what My Son Jesus taught.
These lessons are fundamental to your living in God, so when you see your fellow man, look to see how you can help, how you can love, and then you will find how you can become a true follower of Jesus My Son.

After you receive you must give,
After you give you will receive.
Receive My gifts, give them to others, and then receive
again.

Lord Jesus—6/29/95

As the blood dripped from My crown of thorns and
ran into My eyes, all I could see was the love
I had for mankind.
As the soldiers beat Me and humiliated Me, all I could
feel was the forgiveness I had for mankind.
As the nails drove into My flesh and My body filled
with pain, all I could give was My ever loving heart.
Mankind should look and see the love that flowed from
My heart as a merciful act of forgiveness and wash
themselves in it to cleanse their souls.

A crowd gathered to see a prophet,
A crowd gathered to be healed,
A crowd gathered to listen to the Word.
Today mankind needs to gather as it did in Galilee
to see, to listen, and to be healed.
Today mankind needs to understand that its needs are
the same today as then and that the answer is
the same today as then...the answer is Jesus.

Our Lady—6/29/95

If you look to the heart of Jesus, you will find peace.
If you look to the heart of Jesus, you will find strength.
If you look to the heart of Jesus, you will find hope.

The peaceful rest in Jesus' heart will strengthen you
in times of need.
The strong hope in Jesus' heart will bring you peace
in times of turmoil.
The strength in Jesus' heart will fill you with peaceful
hope in the Lord.

Archangel Raphael—6/29/95

Underneath the emotional, find the spiritual. When you find that, you find the answers to eternal life.

You must look with your spirit not your eyes, and to look spiritually, you must immerse yourself in prayer and meditation on the most Holy Sacrament of the Eucharist.

Open your mind with deep thought on the mystery of the Lord's body in the most holy bread of Communion.

Open your heart by letting that overwhelming feeling of love engulf you; do not block it, do not stop it; just let it flow through you.

Open your spirit in the Sacraments, and open the way of letting God's gifts to you become stronger.

Do these things and grow in God's love. I give you my love and watch over you always. In God's name I bless you, and in God's name I offer you this help.

Lord Jesus—6/29/95

Now you see, now you feel, now you become.

As you see the truth you begin to feel the wonderful joy that is the love of God, and you become one with God.

The light shines on all people; it is there for all.

The light can fill all people; it is there for all.

The light can cure all people; it is there for all.

All people need to accept this and then the light will shine brightly in them.

Healing hearts, healing souls, healing bodies; The Lord heals all.

Repairing hearts, repairing souls, repairing bodies; The Lord repairs all.

Forgiving hearts, forgiving souls, forgiving bodies; The Lord forgives all. Only ask in truth and humility and the Lord will hear and answer.

A circle of love, the Rosary.

A circle of sharing, the Rosary.

A circle of unity, the Rosary.

When you pray the Rosary, pray it with love and accept My love.

When you pray the Rosary, share in My life and share in My love.

When you pray the Rosary, unite with Me and be united in love.

The Rosary, a wonderful gift from My Mother to her children.

A gift that saves, and a gift that brings children home.

God the Father—7/2/95

Unto Him give the glory.

Unto Him give the praise.

Unto Him give the thanks.

The Lord Jesus, God and man.

The Lord Jesus, Spirit and flesh.

The Lord Jesus, truth and light.

Lord Jesus—7/2/95

A follower of Mine one day asked, "What is the way to achieve eternal life?"

The reply was the same then as it is now, "I am the Way." As I am the way, and the Eucharistic bread is My body, then this says that the Sacrament of Communion with Me is the way.

To receive My body in love brings Me to you and you to Me and the more you come to Me, the closer to Heaven you are.

See My body as the way to Heaven and receive it, worship it, and adore it as often as you can.

Vision after Communion of Jesus with His hand outstretched calling me to Him. As I came closer Jesus became the Host and I entered inside it. Inside it was red, and then I saw that it was Jesus' heart. All around were children and angels. Jesus said, "There is a place in My heart for all. Make a place in your heart for all." The angels then were all around me and I could see millions of people in Jesus' heart.

Lord Jesus—7/2/95

Shine in spirit, shine in soul, shine in the Sacraments.

To brighten your spirit and to lift your soul, receive the Sacraments.

To brighten your soul and lift your spirit, receive the Sacraments.

When you receive the Sacraments, you receive God and so you light up your very being.

When I walked this planet, I looked upon many who were sick...sick in spirit, sick in mind, and sick in body.

When I healed, I healed first the spirit and then the mind or body.

If the spirit is healed, then the rest follows; if the spirit is healed then the mind and body are at peace and are ready to be healed.

Sometimes the spirit is unable to accept the healing because the mind is so confused. If this is so, then the mind has to be brought to understand that the turmoil within is what stops God's healing.

The turmoil often is caused by a life lived away from God, a life of disbelief in God, a life not trusting in God.

To be healed, My children need to open their hearts to God.

To be saved, My children need to open their minds to God. And, to be united in eternal bliss, My children need to offer their love to God.

God the Father—7/3/95

Waiting in peace, waiting in love, waiting in hope.
All who wait to receive My Son's body should wait
  like this.

Lord Jesus—7/3/95

My body leads to Heaven,
My body leads to eternal joy,
My body leads to the Father,
The Eucharist...My body, My gift to mankind.

Through the mist, comes the light,
Through the lies, comes the truth,
Through the evil, comes the Lord.
Let God clear the mist of lies that the evil one covers
  mankind's souls with.
Let My love, the love of the Lord Jesus in the Eucharist,
  shine the light into the dark and bring the truth
  into hearts.

Lord Jesus—7/4/95

Filled with love,
Filled with truth,
Filled with God, when you receive My body.

Filled with hope,
Filled with joy,
Filled with God, when you receive My body.

Filled with charity,
Filled with faith,
Filled with God, when you receive My body.

The more you receive My body, the more you are filled
  and the more you have to share.

God the Father—7/5/95

Father of man, Father of creation, Father of Jesus.
The Father of man created all for Jesus, through Jesus
    and in Jesus.

A step taken wisely, can lead to success.
A step taken in love, will lead to success.
A step taken for God, cannot fail.
Step forth for God in love and in wisdom.

Praise those who help,
Praise those who listen, and
Praise those who do My will.

God the Father—7/6/95

Drawing from your heart and giving to others.
Drawing from your soul and helping others.
Drawing from your spirit and strengthening others.
This is what you must do.
Your heart, soul, and spirit are filled with My graces
And so use these to help strengthen others in My
    love.

Finding pain in others and healing it,
Finding confusion in others and clearing it,
Finding hurt in others and comforting it.
Do this for Me through My Son Jesus, and with the
    Holy Spirit.

One day you will see all with eyes of love.
Even in those moments when others cause you pain,
    you will see them only in love.
It is difficult at times to be this way, but you will
    find as time passes it will become easier.
Those who cause the pain do not understand what
    they do, and so they must be forgiven and loved.

Never hold anything against people.

Always forgive, always love, and always smile, for you have a lovely smile that brings joy to others.

Lord Jesus—7/6/95

In the bread find life, in life find love, and in love find God.

I am, I was and I always will be.
I am the Son of God,
I was sacrificed for mankind,
And I always will be there to help.

(About a face I keep seeing.)

My friend, try to understand what you see; see it with eyes of love.

You see many things and know what most are, but some it takes you time to know.

If you see in My face another, then know he comes from Me.

Know he is My servant and friend. He is My loyal subject who gave his all for Me. He is My true follower whose love is known throughout the world, whose faith in God brought him to eternal joy.

His faith is the rock on which I built My Church.

He is the true follower of Jesus Christ who shed his blood for God in Rome, and set in place the authority of God on earth, by passing the keys of Heaven onto his successor.

He is My rock and upon him I build My Church.

He is the one who watches you in love.

God the Father—7/7/95

Bring love to all, bring truth to all, bring faith to all,

And in this way, strengthen yourself in these.

Finding love in others, finding truth in others, finding faith in others, helps you find these in yourself.

Praising love in others, praising truth in others, praising faith in others, helps you praise these in you.

Finding the way to bring praise to God, is by praising God's gifts in you and in others.

Lord Jesus—7/7/95

Vision of truth, vision of joy, vision of grace.

After Communion Jesus came to me and offered me His hand and said, "Come with Me." I entered a round white disk, which I then recognized as the Host. As we entered we were in Heaven. All around were angels and saints smiling at me, and when they touched me I felt so happy.

Jesus kept walking holding my hand and I realized we were going to the Father. I dropped to the ground saying, "I am not worthy," and feeling so unclean. Jesus pulled me along gently, but I would not get up.

As we came to the Father I couldn't look at Him because I felt embarrassed about all the wrong I had done. Jesus said to the Father, "Here is a gift of love I offer to You."

A white light shone from the Father and covered me. I still wouldn't get up, as I was so ashamed of myself. The light filled me with ecstasy. Jesus said, "You are worthy." I still could not look up as I felt so embarrassed at my sins and I felt so small.

Lord Jesus—7/7/95 (after Exposition)

Watching with Me, is a special gift I treasure,
Waiting with Me, is a special time I treasure,
Walking with Me, is a special grace I offer.
Wait and watch with Me to strengthen you for the walk ahead.

31.

Lord   Jesus—7/8/95

All glory and praise to God,
All thanks and worship to God,
All honor and sanctity to God,
All humility and service for God,
All giving and welcoming for God,
All loving and sharing for God,
All to God for His glory,
All from you in love.

Truth of truths, Jesus in the Host,
Love of loves, Jesus in the Host,
God of God, Jesus in the Host.
The truth and the love of God are to be found in
  the Host.

Until the end, I Am.
From the beginning, I was.
Always, I will be.

Find peace in My body,
Find comfort in My heart,
Find love in My soul,
Find it all in the Eucharist.

A follower of Mine one day answered the question that
  so many ask, "Who are You?"
Peter answered in the truth of God, "You are the Messiah,
  You are the Son of God."
The truth spoken by Peter is the same truth you must
  speak, the truth that is God.

St.   Peter—7/8/95

A long time ago I was there, but you did not recognize
  me. You looked, you saw, but you did not know.
  Know me now and join with me in singing the

praises of the Lord God Jesus Christ, the true Messiah, the true Lord, and the true God.

Jesus, who with the Father and the Holy Spirit is the true God. Our Lord, our Savior, our Redeemer, our Friend, our God. Jesus, who wept from His heart for mankind, wept tears of blood and tears of love. Jesus, who loved completely His family on earth, loved all, no matter who or what they were. Jesus, who saved all, not just a few. Jesus, my Lord, my God, my Master, and my dearest friend, whose forgiveness knows no end. Jesus, who says to all, "Become My new apostles and follow Me."

Lord Jesus—7/9/95

To talk in My name, means to talk in love.
To heal in My name, means to heal with love.
To comfort in My name, means to comfort through love.

The opposite to live is evil,
So to oppose evil is to live.

Comforting, loving, and caring for souls is what I did while on earth, and continue to do throughout eternity.
This is what you should do with your time on earth in My name, the name of Jesus.
Then spend eternity in love with Me.

Holy Spirit—7/9/95

Saints and angels sing praises to God.
All the heavens glorify God.
Eternally God is thanked by the very existence of His creation.
Mankind, as part of God's creation, glorifies God, and mankind, even though it may not know it, thanks God every time it performs an act of true love.
Mankind, the saints of the future, and the children of God.

Archangel Raphael—7/10/95

Praise God for His love,
Praise God for His mercy,
Praise God for His forgiveness.

Honor the Lord for His love,
Honor the Lord for His sacrifice,
Honor the Lord for His saving grace.

Worship the Spirit for His love,
Worship the Spirit for His truth,
Worship the Spirit for His strength.

Adore God for His merciful forgiveness, which shows His love.
Adore God for His saving grace of His sacrifice, which shows His love.
Adore God for His strength found in His truth, which shows His love.

Lord Jesus—7/10/95

Drops of blood run from My wounds, and become a river of saving grace.
All My children need to wash their souls in this river, and they can do this through the Sacraments.
The Sacraments are My saving graces and so they are My love.

Friendship, truth, and love.
Faith, hope, and charity.
Jesus, Father, and the Holy Spirit.
All one,
All of God,
All God.

God the Father—7/11/95

To rest after work is necessary,
To recuperate after toil is needed,
To recover after taking the burden on your shoulders
is important.
Rest in Me, and let Me lift your burden.

God the Father—7/13/95

Truth is always there, you just need to follow it.
Love is always there, you just need to want it.
Hope is always there, you just need to believe it.
Jesus Christ is always there, you just need to trust
in Him.
Jesus Christ is always there, you just need to ask
of Him.
Jesus Christ is always there, you just need to seek
Him.
Jesus is the truth that is the hope that is found
when you seek God, for Jesus is God.

Truth is not always what you see,
Truth is not always what you hear,
Truth is not always what you know.
When you know the complete truth you will be with
Me.
Until then accept that sometimes you make mistakes
and then correct them.

God the Father—7/14/95

Sharing in pain means sharing in love.

Lord Jesus—7/15/95

Walking along the way is a difficult walk.
Often there are, what seem like failures,
but they are really successes.

Lord Jesus—7/15/95

Divinity revealed on the cross.
Divinity revealed with the resurrection.
Divinity revealed with the ascension.
The true Son of God died on the cross,
Was resurrected from the dead, ascended into Heaven.
All revealed, I am divine,
All revealed, God does exist,
All revealed, the power of God's love.

God the Father—7/16/95

All praise and glory to God.
All worship and honor to God.
All thanks and love to God.
Honor the Father,
Glorify the Holy Spirit,
Love the Lord Jesus through your praise and worship,
Thank the one true God.

A flower, a rose, a sweet fragrance...the love of Jesus.
A rock, a pillar, a fortress...the love of Jesus.
A gift, a grace, a joy...the love of Jesus.
There for all, there for you, there forever.

Enjoying family and friends is a special joy,
    but remember, all of mankind is your family.

Lord Jesus—7/16/95

Within, feel My love,
Within, feel My joy,
Within, feel My fire,
The fire of love that is a joy found in the Eucharist.

God the Father—7/17/95

Being part of My family means being a brother, a
father, a son to all.

Work for God is the most important work.
Work for God is the most difficult work.
Work for God is the most rewarding work,
For it is the work of saving souls.

Lord Jesus—7/17/95

Along the way you will find many who need your time.
Along the way you will find many who need your love.
Along the way you will find many who need your strength.
Offer it freely, offer it with love, and offer it in My
name.

Place your heart into Mine,
Place your spirit into Mine,
Place your soul into Mine,
Become one with Me and become My love.

God the Father—7/18/95

Praying strengthens, praying fills, praying brings you
closer to God.
To find strength pray and fill yourself with God's love.

Lord Jesus—7/18/95

Love, truth, faith,
Hope, charity, forgiveness,
Jesus, Father, Holy Spirit.
One in love, one in hope, one in God.
The only truth, the only charity, the only God,

37.

The Redeemer, the Creator, the Paraclete.
Lord Jesus—7/18/95

Times goes by, but here am I,
Time rolls on, but I am still the Son,
Time passes, but I still give My graces.
Eternally I am here, eternally I am the Son, and
Eternally I give My graces.

Lord Jesus—7/19/95

When you take My body within,
You take My whole being within.
When you take My body within,
You take My spirit within.
When you take My body within,
You take My truth within.
I am the truth that brings your spirit into being.

†††

*C*hapter 4.

Accept My Love

Lord Jesus—7/19/95

Throughout time I have offered My love, and few accept it. Most turn their back on God, and live life as if that is all there is. Most just live for the moment that is life, and because of this deny their spirit its opportunity to become what it was meant to be.

Life is just a second in the eternal clock of true existence. Life needs to be seen as what it truly is, it is the time that each person can show his love of God, of others, and of all God's creations. By doing this, he then becomes what he was created to be, a spirit of love.

While My soul weeps tears of the Spirit, My heart weeps tears of love.

While My body aches with the pain of man's sins, My heart aches with the forgiveness I have for all.

While My spirit is wounded by the scorn of mankind, My heart is wounded to let My mercy flow out freely to all.

My little one come to Me with your troubles and I will lift them.

Come to Me with your struggles and I will strengthen you.

Come to Me in love and I will fill you, for I love you.

God the Father—7/20/95

My Son Jesus lays His life before all mankind as an example of how to live and how to reach eternal happiness. All mankind should look to what Jesus said, how Jesus acted, and how Jesus worshipped His Father in Heaven. If mankind can look to Jesus and follow His example, then life on earth will be as it was meant to be and Heaven will welcome many home.

Lord Jesus—7/20/95

To do My work, you need My body daily,
To do My work, you need My love always,
To do My work, you need My strength within you.
When you receive My body daily, you are filled with
My love and My strength in abundance, then you
can share it with others in need.

Smell of roses at Our Lady's statue in Our Lady of Victories Church.

God the Father—7/20/95

Fragrance of love, fragrance of joy,
Fragrance of beauty, Mary, Mother of God.

Lord Jesus—7/22/95

What a feeling, a feeling of sadness that you may
have hurt your Lord.
What a sadness, a sadness that makes you feel offensive.
What a joy, a joy you bring Me because you show
you truly love Me.

To speak the truth is to speak in love,
To speak the truth is to speak in kindness,
To speak the truth is to speak in humility.

Speaking the truth means to show love, kindness, humility, for in this way you show the truth of God.
Our Lady—7/23/95

Home of homes, Heaven
Peace of peaces, Jesus
Truth of truths, God.

A family of love is what all families should be.
A family of truth is what all families should be.
A family of God is what all families should try to be.

Lord Jesus—7/23/95

Receive and give, give and receive.
Receive My love and give your love to others.
Give your love to others and receive My love.

God the Father—7/24/95

Followers of Jesus are sons and daughters of mine.
Followers of Jesus are true to God.
Followers of Jesus are future saints.
When you follow Jesus you become My children, and when you remain true to God you become saints.

Lord Jesus—7/24/95

Do My work in love, in truth, and in Me,
Then nothing can go wrong.
Trust Me, trust My Father, and trust My Spirit.

God the Father—7/25/95

In church, come to Me with your heart wanting My love.
In church, come to Me with your soul seeking My peace.

41.

In church, come to Me with your spirit searching for
My graces.
Come and be filled to overflowing, come and be filled
to give, come and be filled to love.

Lord Jesus—7/26/95

Find your strength in Me,
Find your protection in Me,
Find your destiny in Me.
The strength that comes from My body,
The protection that comes from My love,
The destiny that comes from your faith.

Through the pain on the cross, I forgave all of mankind's
sins,
Through the suffering on the cross, I lifted all of
mankind's sins from them.
Through the terrible torture on the cross, I released
mankind from the bondage of evil it has welcomed.
Opening My heart on the cross, I united Myself with
mankind's heart so that we could become one in
eternity.

From your heart take your love and give to those in
need.
From your heart take your love and offer to those
wanting.
From your heart take your love and see the gift I
gave you to give to others.

Just take a rest with Me,
Just take a break with Me,
Just take a time alone with Me,
Be with Me and be filled with My love.

Walking with My love in your heart, makes the path
easier. Walking with My joy in your soul, makes the
path happy. Walking with My fire in your spirit, makes
the path a true pleasure.

Under My shadow find love,
Under My shadow find peace,
Under My shadow find truth.
The love that leads to true peace, the love of God.

Lord Jesus—7/29/95

Follow your heart and follow Me, for I am in your heart.
Follow your heart and you follow love, for I put My love there.
Follow your heart and follow truth, for I placed My truth there.
The truthful way your heart leads you is a loving way...the way of Jesus.

Trust is so important,
Hope is so necessary,
Truth is so obvious.
When you trust in God it is important that you place all your hopes in His hands. This is necessary so that the truth can become obvious.

Lord Jesus—7/30/95

The sweetness of love turns to pain, when the love is ignored.
The sweetness of love turns to beauty, when the love is nurtured.
The sweetness of love turns to everlasting joy, when the love is treasured.

Lord Jesus—8/1/95

In love all is possible,
In love all can be,
In love all awaits,
I am love, so find all in Me.

43.

Around the world all people are different only in appearance and traditions. All people are the same within, with the same needs, the same hopes, and the same truths. It is only how they respond to these, which separates one person from another. To respond in love is the bond that unites the family of man, to respond in selfishness is what tears mankind apart.

Lord Jesus—8/3/95

A flower opens in your heart, the flower that is My love.
A flower opens in My heart, the flower that is your love.
A flower opens in our hearts, the flower of love that unites us forever.

Lord Jesus—8/4/95

Just a short walk with Me will lead you to eternity.
Just a brief moment in My love brings you to Heaven above.
Just a simple faith in your life takes you to an eternity of delight.

God the Father—8/5/95

Fruit of love, Jesus,
Fruit of hope, Jesus,
Fruit of truth, Jesus.
Eternal fruit of love that brings hope to those who are in need of the truth.

God the Father—8/6/95

A son has a special relationship with his father.
A son has a special love for his father.
A son has a special bond with his father.
A son and his father united by a love which bonds their relationship forever.

God the Father—8/6/95

The body and the blood,
The agony and the ecstasy,
The giving and the receiving,
The Lord Jesus gave His body in agony so that mankind
could receive eternal ecstasy.
The Lord Jesus shed His blood so that mankind could
see the agony that sin causes, and receive the
forgiveness that God gave.
The Lord Jesus gave His body and blood in agony
and offers it in the Eucharist as a path to never-
ending ecstasy that all can receive if they truly seek
it.

God the Father—8/7/95

Keeping love in your heart means keeping Jesus there.
Keeping love in your heart means denying none.
Keeping love in your heart means opening your heart
to all.
Jesus showed how, in His life, and in His death, when
he denied evil and opened His heart to all.

Lord Jesus—8/7/95

Under My protection you are safe, just believe.
Under My love you are protected, just believe.
Under My shadow you are strengthened, just believe.
Believe and it is so, and it is only doubt that stops
its being.

If you listen to your heart, you will find My guiding
hand.
If you listen to your heart, you will find My loving
word there.
If you listen to your heart, you will find Me there
waiting to help.
Listen to your heart and listen to Me.

Lord Jesus—8/8/95

Try to see from your heart not your mind,
   then you see with love.
Try to see from your heart not your reason,
   then you see the truth.
Try to see from your heart not your preconceived ideas,
   then you see as you should.
See in love and truth, and see how things should
   be.

From within your heart, see others,
From within your soul, feel for others,
From within your self, want to help others.
Within are the answers you seek,
For I am within.

To eat with Me means to fill yourself of Me so that
   you then can fill others.

One cloudy day I sat and talked to a crowd that
had come to listen. As I talked drops of rain began
to fall, and as they did many ran for cover while
others stayed and listened. Those who stayed knew
the rain could not harm them and that the word of
God was with them.

Today mankind needs to understand that the word
of God is still with them, and if they stay close to
it nothing can harm them. All will be as drops of
rain (just harmlessly falling down).

During the pain, I saw love,
During the torture, I saw hope,
During the agony, I saw faith.
I saw the love of those with faith, and I saw the
   hope in their hearts.

Hanging alone on the cross I saw the whole of
mankind before Me. I saw their weaknesses, pain,
suffering and sins. I saw it all and I forgave.

With the giving of My life to the Father, all that I saw was forgiven, all were redeemed. I carried all of mankind's errors to the grave and when I was resurrected I left them there.

Mankind, however, keeps trying to dig them up, to resurrect them. Mankind needs to accept My forgiveness and leave its sins where they belong, dead and buried in the grave.

Compassion comes from the heart,
Compassion comes with love,
Compassion comes when you understand mankind's weaknesses.

As time goes by, so does the chance of redemption.

God the Father—8/10/95

At times such as these, many need to rethink their faith. Are they ones with a faith of convenience or with a true faith? A faith of convenience is a faith that says, "I believe only what agrees with my lifestyle, my needs, and my pride. Anything else I will ignore. I will only receive the Sacraments when I want...once a year is enough so that I can keep my obligation. I will only attend Mass at special occasions; I don't need to go at other times. Anyway, I don't have the time."

This is a faith of convenience which really is no faith at all. It is a faith that is kept as an insurance policy just in case there is a God.

A true faith is a faith that believes, follows, and honors God completely. A true faith receives the Sacraments often, attends Mass often, accepts all of God's commandments, not just a few. How many today have a true faith? Not many.

All now need to look and see which faith they have and to make an effort to have true faith, the true faith that leads to Heaven.

My Son gives His life as a never-ending sacrifice that lifts the sins of mankind from their souls, if only they believe and accept.

47.

Lord Jesus—8/10/95

Praising God is a gift, a gift from God to you which
   you return to God.
Loving God is a grace, a grace from God to you which
   you return to God.
Working for God is a joy, a joy from God to you
   which you return to God.
Return to God all He gives, and He gives you more.

God the Father—8/11/95

Finding peace of spirit, means finding Jesus.
Finding hope, hope of the future, means finding Jesus.
Finding truth, the only truth, means finding Jesus.
Jesus is the true peace that answers every hope.

When you are down, be lifted in the sweet body of
   Jesus.
When you are low, be raised in the sweet blood of
   Jesus.
When you are sad, be happy in the Sacrament of
   Jesus' body and blood.

Lord Jesus—8/11/95

Trust in Me, that is all you need to do,
Trust in Me and be true.

Trust in Me, that is all you need in your heart,
Trust in Me and never part.

Trust in Me, that is all you need in your life,
Trust in Me and have no strife.

Trust is so important for it shows your love.

Running a race and jumping hurdles, you do not look back to see how many hurdles you have knocked over. You keep going, but change your stride so as not to knock any more over.

With sins, it is the same. Once you are forgiven, do not keep looking back and worrying over them. Keep going, but change your life so as not to sin again.

Lord Jesus—8/12/95

Under a bush was a bird hiding and frightened. Its fear was of the men all around, whom it thought wanted to injure it. Then a hand of love was offered to the bird. It could feel the peace and comfort that flowed from that hand. It was My hand coming to save it from its fears. As it placed itself into the hand of God, it was lifted from its hiding place and set free to fly in beauty.

It is the same with mankind. Many keep their true selves hidden, frightened of those around them. It is when they accept the hand of love that I (Jesus) offer them, that they can become free and show the true beauty that is their spirit.

God the Father—8/13/95

Seeing with eyes of love means loving all, regardless.

Faith, a little word that means everything,
Faith, a little word that brings everything,
Faith, a little word that is everything.
Have faith, and everything is there for you.

Lord Jesus—8/13/95

My Mother, your Mother, everyone's Mother.
So sweet, so pure, so loving,
So human, so special, so chosen.

49.

God the Father—8/14/95

Words of love become love,
Words of love are love,
Words of love stay forever.

Lord Jesus—8/14/95

Enjoying life means loving God,
Loving life means enjoying God.

Our Lady—8/15/95 (Assumption Day)

Lifted to Heaven in love,
Lifted to Heaven in body,
Lifted to Heaven in God's glory.

When I was taken home to Heaven by my Son,
it was a glorious day. I was filled with love throughout
my body, and with this love I was assumed to the
Father in Heaven.

Lord Jesus—8/15/95

Mother's arms are open wide,
Mother's arms are open to all,
Mother's arms are waiting for all.

My Mother in Heaven with Me,
My Mother in Heaven as Queen,
My Mother in Heaven in God's glory,

Mother of all in need,
Mother of all in hope,
Mother of all regardless.

In early times, Mother believed,
In early times, Mother answered the call,
In early times, Mother showed the beauty of her love.

Lord Jesus—8/15/95

Just trust, wait and see, and believe in Me.

God the Father—8/17/95

I am, I was, and I always will be,
The Father, the Son, and the Spirit,
The Trinity, the One, the Only.

A man will always see and hear what he wants to,
while he has pride.

Praying can be done quietly,
Praying can be done silently,
Praying can be done anywhere.

Prayers of love are the best type of prayer.
Prayers of joy are the nicest type of prayer,
Prayers of humility are the truest type of prayer.
Pray in love joyfully, and be humble in your love.

One day a man with a heart filled with the fire
of God stepped forth to proclaim the coming of the
Savior. This man proclaimed to all who would listen
that the Son of God was coming. He called for repentance
and returning to the love of God.

Today, look and see the messages from the Mother
of Jesus. They are the same. She asks the same as
John, and she gives the same warnings. Does not
mankind see the similarities? Does not mankind
understand what is being asked of it and why? Look
now to John the Baptist and see what he proclaimed
and then what happened. Then look at what your
Mother proclaims today and wonder at what is to follow.

Under the hard outer layers that some have, you
will find the love that all have. Sometimes this love
is hidden so deep it seems it isn't there, but it still
is.

My Son gives His life for mankind in an eternal sacrifice that echoes throughout time. The blood that was shed for mankind flows as a river of true love and forgiveness. The blood of Jesus became the cleansing grace that defeated evil. The blood still is there waiting to cleanse all those who bring themselves to be freed by Jesus' love.

Jesus, true love,
Jesus, true man,
Jesus, true God.

Divine love,
Diving man,
Divinity.

When you look upon the body of Jesus in the Sacrament of the Eucharist, see His love.
When you look upon the blood of Jesus in the Sacrament, see His mercy.
When you look upon the bread, see the body and blood there for you, there in love and Mercy.

A man can be love, or he can be hate.
A man can be true, or he can be false.
A man can be kind, or he can be cruel.
The choice is man's, but the rewards are God's,
The rewards of Heaven, or the suffering of hell.
Make the right choice and receive the right rewards.

After love comes life and after life comes love.
Life came from God's love and returns to God's love.

A loving heart, a loving spirit,
A loving man, Jesus.

A loving being, a loving gift,
A loving Son, Jesus.

A loving truth, a loving grace,
Loving God, Jesus.

Broken in spirit, broken in heart,
Broken in soul, every time mankind sins.

Filled with love, filled with joy,
Filled with glory, every time mankind turns to God.

God the Father—8/18/95

Filling your heart with love,
Filling your heart with peace,
Filling your heart with Jesus in the Sacraments.

Waiting patiently is a virtue,
Waiting patiently is a gift,
Waiting patiently is a grace.

Vision after Communion of a bunch of red roses, from which Jesus took one and put in my hands, saying "I love you, share in My love." The other roses were all the people in the world whom Jesus loves.

Lord Jesus—8/19/95

On a mountain one day came a man who loved God, but did not know it. He came because he had heard that God was there; he came in search of God. This man saved his people and led them to their promised land. This man was a true man of God.

Today there is a mountain to climb to find God, it is the mountain of faith; you must climb this mountain. There is a mountain to overcome, it is the mountain of self; you must overcome this mountain. There is a mountain to move, it is the mountain of sin; you must move this mountain. When this is done you will find many saved and led home to their promised land.

Return unto God what is His,
Return unto God your love,
Return unto God your life,
And in return, receive God's love.

Saving all mankind with My sacrifice,
Loving all mankind with My heart,
Filling all mankind with My hope.

Prayers are like perfume to My heart,
Prayers have such a sweet aroma,
Prayers bring a bouquet of love to Me.

53.

God the Father—8/20/95

To travel closer to My love, take the path of the
  Sacraments.
To travel closer to My heart, take the way that is
  Jesus.
To travel closer to God, take the journey that is found
  in the Sacraments that lead you to Jesus, for He
  is God.

Lord Jesus—8/20/95

Come to Me in love,
Come to Me in wanting,
Come to Me in joy,
When you want My love, it brings Me joy, so come
  to Me often.

*At Charismatic Mass in Adelaide, saw wounds bleeding
on the knees of Jesus on the cross.*

Drops of love,
Dew of mercy,
Dawn of peace.

God the Father—8/21/95

In the beginning, man knew God,
At present, most do not know God,
In the end, all will know God.

Lord Jesus—8/21/95

When you take My love within, you start to become
  My love.
When you take My body within, you start to become
  My body.
When you take My heart into your heart, you become
  My body on earth which shows My love to all.

*Vision after Communion of set of steps leading to
Heaven's golden gates. Each step was taken when I
received Communion. As I took Communion each time,
Jesus appeared and helped me up a step. He said,
"Taking My body within, brings you a step closer to
Heaven."*

Lord Jesus—8/22/95

A cold heart makes a sad spirit.
A warm heart makes a happy spirit.
A hot heart makes a strong soul.
A heart on fire with the love of God burns so hot
that it can warm even the coldest of hearts.

Life is a gift, and like all gifts it should be appreciated
and enjoyed.
Life is a journey, and like all journeys it needs a
clear destination so that the way can be planned.
Life is a time of wonderful adventure, and like all
adventures it has to be shared to make it worthwhile.
Share your life with Jesus, and find the journey becomes
a wonderful adventure that you will enjoy.

When you sit with Me, I sit with you,
When you sit with Me, I am happy,
When you sit with Me, I fill you with My love.

Moments of love,
Moments of joy,
Moments of hope.

Moments of God,
Moments of Jesus,
Moments of the Spirit.

The love of God seen in the joy of Jesus and brought
alive in the hope of the Spirit.

God the Father—8/23/95

Thorns of love pierced My Son's skin.
As thorns of hate they were given, but thorns of love
they became.
It is the way of love, to turn hate into beauty and
to turn pain into joy.

To worry is unnecessary,
To fret is not worthwhile,
To be anxious is useless,
To trust in Jesus is the answer to all your worries,
So do not fret, do not be anxious. Just trust in Jesus.

55.

(About prayer for others)

Pray from your heart,
Pray from your soul,
Pray from your spirit,
Touch others through your prayer of love that
    touches hearts, saves souls, and strengthens spirits.

God the Father—8/24/95

Praise the Lord in all you do,
Praise the Lord in all you say,
Praise the Lord in all you share.
When you do God's work, you share God's love and
    you must say this to all.

*After Communion, vision of Jesus' heart which broke
in half to expose the host within.*

Lord Jesus—8/24/95

To accept in love all that is put upon you, is the
    way of love.
To accept in love all that is asked of you, is the
    way of Jesus.
To accept in Jesus all that is required of you, is
    the way to Heaven.

From My heart I give,
From My heart I embrace,
From My heart I love.
I love to give My children gifts that will bring them
    to embrace My love.

God the Father—8/25/95

A Father, a friend, a true love.
A Father, a companion, a true help.
A Father, a partner, a true strength.
Along the way, your Father becomes your friend and
    companion.
Along the way your Father becomes your partner, who
    longs to help by giving you His strength and love.

Lord Jesus—8/25/95

As I lay on the cross, I only thought of love.
As I gave My life, I only showed love.
As I returned to life, I only brought love.
This is how mankind must be: only thinking of love,
    only showing love, and only bringing love.

When My friends call, I answer,
When My friends call, I love,
When My friends call, I am there.

Lord Jesus—8/26/95

   *Vision after Communion of Jesus' hands holding His
heart and offering it to me saying, "I give you My heart."*

In times of stress, look for My peace,
In times of frustration, look to My heart,
In times of dismay, look to My love.
Find your peace in My heart when you are filled with
    My love.

Building on love, is building on firm foundations.
Building on love, is the true building block of life.
Building on love, is the only way to build for eternal
    life.

Write the truth,
Tell the truth,
And live the truth.

God the Father—8/27/95

Prayer is the answer to all,
Prayer is the strength for all,
Prayer is the gift offered to all.

Hope springs eternal from the eternal spring of life.

One day, one moment, your life.
One God, one body, your Lord.
One day your life became God's, and in that one moment
    you joined the body of Jesus.

57.

When you love, you are filled with joy.
When you love Me, I am filled with joy.
When you love others, they are filled with joy.
The joy that comes from God is catching, for it catches
   My children and brings them to Me.

Lord Jesus—8/27/95

The time of hope is here; hope in Jesus.
The time of love is here; love of Jesus.
The time of truth is here; truth that is Jesus.

God the Father—8/28/95

Never assume, never prejudge.
Always think the best, always love.
In this way, you show the true spirit of Christ.

Lord Jesus—8/28/95

The joy you have is for all, but do all want it?
The joy you have is to be made known to all so
   all will want it.
The joy you have is a grace, a grace of My love,
   a love for all.

To look in love, is the only way to look,
To give in love, is the only way to give,
To offer in love, is the only way to offer.
Give your love to those looking for help.
Offer your love to those lost and looking.

†††

Chapter 5.

In Search Of God

God the Father—8/29/95

One day a man came in search of God. This man climbed a mountain and found love; he found God. The mountain he climbed was not only physical, but also a spiritual mountain. Once he reached the top he saw there was still so much higher to go, higher into the love of God.

This man gave himself completely to God and in so doing became a special man, a man who would serve his God, and in so doing serve his people. This man brought the family of God to its promised land. He brought them in complete obedience to God, but they in their pride often tried to deny God. God through His servant and friend showed them many miracles and wonders, but even then many still denied God. They built false idols, idols of self, of sin, of corruption; so many idols. God in His mercy continued to show His love of His children through His servant.

He gave His family the Ten Commandments for all to live by so eternal life in Heaven could be achieved. When God gave the commandments, they showed how God wanted His children to live, commandments of love, commandments not to hurt, but to help, commandments of life. The commandments were just that, commandments, not suggestions. Mankind should look and see if it is following these commandments, and if not, why? The commandments are the true way to live... there is no other way.

When God sent Himself in His Son Jesus to lead His family back to the promised land, He showed how to live the commandments and He gave a new commandment, "To love one another as I have loved you." How many more times will mankind have to be told plainly and with no double meanings how to live, how to reach Heaven? How many more times before mankind listens?

Lord Jesus—8/29/95

When My family becomes one family in love then they will come to understand the love of God. It is then that mankind will wonder why it did not embrace the true way of life before.

Isn't this the way of mankind, seeing the truth only after most have experienced it? What a change mankind needs to undergo, a change that brings faith.

A river flows, a river of love,
A river runs, a river of grace,
A river overflows, a river of forgiveness.
Enter the river and be filled with the graces of love
    and forgiveness; the river that is Jesus.

Times of love bring times of joy.
Times of love bring times of peace.
Times of love bring times of hope.
The time of peaceful hope comes joyfully to those who
    love God.

God the Father—8/30/95

Of those who followed My Son, there is a special woman,
    a woman whose life was one of joy, of happiness,
    of love.
Her life showed the world how as humans we could
    be, how life can be.
This woman so special, so sweet.
This woman with Jesus from the beginning and by
    His side for eternity.
This woman who by her sacrifice offered her whole
    life as a gift to God.
This woman who is Mary, Mother of God.
This woman who is your Mother.

Vision before Communion of chalice and Host. Jesus said, "Find your peace in My Body and Blood."

Lord Jesus—8/30/95

To eat with Me, is to be at My table,
To be at My table, is to be filled with love,
To be filled with love, is to be filled with Me.

To talk of Me, is to talk of love,
To talk of Me, is to bring love,
To talk of Me, is to love, bringing Me to others.

God the Father—8/31/95

The end and the beginning,
The end of the old and the beginning of the new,
Jesus' life on earth and Jesus' life in you.

Vision after Communion of Jesus on the cross with His heart exposed with the words, "The loving heart of Jesus."

Lord Jesus—8/31/95

The love shown by My Father when He accepted My offering in atonement for mankind's sins is often forgotten. It took a magnificent act of mercy to forgive so much. It took a wonderful act of love to welcome back the fallen, and it took a very special gift to overcome sin; the gift of God on the cross.

God the Father—9/1/95

A change in seasons can be like a change of heart, it can be for better or worse.
A change in seasons can bring warmth and sunshine, or it can bring cold and dark.
A change of heart can be the same, light or dark, good or evil.
The results can be everlasting sunshine or never ending dark.
Make the right change and receive the best reward.

That day in the temple as a child, My Son Jesus brought the Word in scripture alive. He set fire to the souls of those who listened, He increased their love of God. How good it was when later, as an adult, Jesus was helped by one of those who heard Him in the temple as a child. The fire set alight in Nicodemus' soul on that day remained with him throughout life. That fire opened Nicodemus to understand who Jesus truly is.

61.

Lord Jesus—9/1/95

In My heart is only love, love for all,
In My spirit is only joy, joy for all,
In My Father is only mercy, mercy for all.
Open your heart to Mine and receive the joy of the
   Spirit,
Open your heart to Mine and accept the mercy of
   the Father,
Open your heart to Mine and be filled with love.

Lord Jesus—9/2/95

A man worked for himself all his life, and in the
   end all he had was poor health and worry.
A man worked for God all his life, and in the end
   all he had was riches in Heaven and joy for eternity.
A man must make the right choices to receive the
   right rewards.

To worry is unnecessary,
To worry is unwise,
To worry is unworthy.

Find peace within the Eucharist,
Find joy within the Eucharist,
Find hope within the Eucharist.
The Eucharist—food of life, food of love, food of God.

God the Father—9/3/95

In the service of God, all becomes a joy,
In the service of God, all becomes a pleasure,
In the service of God, all becomes your family.

To love God, to work for God, to love your fellow
   man...what else is there in life?

Take My love within,
Take My joy within,
Take My hope within.
Do this when you receive My Son
   in the Eucharist.

Jerusalem the city of My children, the city I loved. Within Jerusalem so many places for the worship of the Father, and so many people filling them. When the Father sent His Son to His people, He sent Him to Jerusalem to show the love of God to mankind and how God's love was shown.

The people who said they loved God were the ones who tortured and killed God's Son. The very people who devoted their lives to God were the ones who persecuted God's only Son. These children turned their back on God's Son as they could not see the truth, for their eyes were covered with pride, a pride that brings anger and hate, a pride that kills, a pride that can destroy souls.

This pride is still with mankind and if God's Son were to come today, do you think it would be any different? Today, as yesterday, some would believe, but many would not. The world today is the same as Jerusalem 2000 years ago, loved by God, but full of pride, a pride that blinds, that fills with anger and hate, a pride that can destroy souls.

Mankind in his pride has come no further spiritually than he was so long ago. Mankind in his pride has stagnated and has become stale. Mankind in pride is lost, wandering the path of life and blinded to where he walks. Remove the pride, embrace humility, and walk the true path that leads to the prize of eternal life in God.

Try to relax, try to rest, try to return to peace. Do not get drawn into the trap of proving your worth, just accept you are worthy. I am there by your side every second, just lean on Me.

Lord Jesus—9/7/95

To receive Me within, is to be filled with My love, a love you can bring to others, a love you can share with others, and a love you can fill others with. The love of God, there for all and all is there from it.

Vision at Communion of Jesus' heart surrounded by red roses. Jesus said, "My heart of love."

Lord Jesus—9/7/95

There was a time when My love was eagerly sought after, when so many people filled the churches and professed their love of God. The churches called to the people and they came, came in search of eternal love. The people were mostly poor, poor in heart, poor in soul, and often poor in goods. What they found within the church was the richness of God's love. When they were touched by this love they felt as if they were princes, they felt full of the treasure of God's love. They felt the intimate caress of God's heart. These people...full of love, full of peace, full of truth. These people...following God in their whole life. These people... a shining example to others.

Now the children of the devout turn away from the inheritance their ancestors gained for them. Now the children do not go to church, do not seek God's love, God's treasure.

What was eagerly sought before by many is now rejected. The early example now needs to be returned to, and the people should return to the church to find the treasure of God's love that is their inheritance.

The truth is the only way to live.
The truth is the only value to have.
The truth is the only hope there is.
I am the truth and to follow My way brings hope
    of life that is to be valued.

God's love is for all; never deny anyone,
God's healing is for all; never refuse anyone, and
God's mercy is for all; so tell them.

†††

Chapter 6.

The Gift of Love

Lord Jesus—9/8/95 (about Blessed Mother's birth)

When this baby was born a new dawn arrived, the dawn that would bring the Son to shine over mankind. When mankind sees the importance of the birth of Mary, My Mother, and understands that her birth was the beginning of the return of mankind to God, then the true relationship of mankind to God can be more easily understood, and mankind can see how it is loved by God.

A beautiful soul,
A beautiful heart,
A beautiful woman, My Mother.
A soul that reflected God, a heart that loved God, and a woman who glorified God.

Carrying the cross on My back, I looked into the crowd and there was My Mother. When our eyes met I could feel her anguish and I could feel her love. With this glance, My heart was filled with the strength of this woman, a pillar of strength, a pillar of love, and a pillar of motherly care.

I looked and returned to her My love, My strength to carry her on. So it is with all mankind when they look to Mother. She gives them her love, her strength, her care, and then she turns their eyes to Jesus so they can be filled with My love and strength to carry them on to Heaven.

65.

Lord Jesus—9/9/95

To love means to forgive,
To love means to forget,
To love means to understand.

To share is to love,
To sacrifice is to love,
To give is to love.
To love means sharing and sacrificing together and for
each other.
To love means forgiving and forgetting the hurt and
pain, and understanding each other.
In this way, you give completely to each other in love,
and so give to God a wonderful gift.

Memories of love, memories of hope, memories of the
way you were.
You loved and hoped in each other, for this is how
you were.
Now you love and hope in Me together, for this is
how you are.

Meeting in love only brings love,
Meeting in joy only brings joy,
Meeting in hope only brings hope.
When you meet in prayer, you bring My love, joy,
and hope into your hearts.

With his children, a father should love them all.
In his love, a father offers gifts to express his feelings,
and a father offers gifts to share his love. If any of
his children do not accept his gifts, a father does
not stop loving them, only tries to find other gifts
or ways of helping.

It is the same for the Father in Heaven. He loves
all of His children the same, and He offers them all
His love. When the children accept His gifts of love,
it brings the Father great joy, but when some only
accept what they think they need or do not accept
any, the Father still loves them the same.

With those children who do not accept all that is
offered and even reject some of the gifts, the Father
increases the gifts they do accept so that they may

open themselves completely to the Lord. This is why many of those who are in churches that deny some of the gifts and teachings offered by God receive in abundance those gifts they do accept.

It is in this way the Father wants to open their hearts to the complete truth of Jesus in the Sacraments, in His Mother, and in His one body, the church. Those who do not accept any of the Father's gifts of love, can be helped by those who do accept and believe, for these are filled to overflowing so that they can share with their brethren whom the Father still loves and wants to welcome home.

They can be helped by prayer and by example to open themselves to God, and those who do the helping will receive in abundance the gifts and graces to do the work. Brother helping brother to be one in God; what a glorious day when this happens.

God the Father—9/10/95

Full of the Spirit, anything is possible. The Holy Spirit is there to give you the gifts I have to offer. The Holy Spirit is always waiting to help, waiting to strengthen, waiting to heal. When you believe this and allow the Spirit to work, then all is possible...just believe!

Spirit of God, spirit of love.
Spirit of God, spirit of freedom.
Spirit of God, spirit of truth.

Spirit of God, one in the Father.
Spirit of God, one in Jesus.
Spirit of God, one in the Trinity.

Spirit of God, light of life.
Spirit of God, fire of Heaven.
Spirit of God, wind of mercy.

Lord Jesus—9/10/95

The way of life is found in Me,
The way of life is found in God,
The way of life is found in God's spirit.

I am the way of life that leads to the Father with the Holy Spirit, to fill you with love.
I, the Father, and the Spirit...the way, the only way.

One God, the only God,
One love, the only love.

God the Father—9/11/95

To find a heart open, is a joy,
To find a heart closed, a sorrow.

To find a willing spirit is wonderful,
To find a denying spirit, a tragedy.

To find a loving soul is a miracle,
To find a hating soul, a sadness.

With an open heart and a willing spirit, a soul can perform miracles.
With a closed heart and a denying spirit, a soul can only be in sadness.
What a tragedy to see such sorrow.

God the Father—9/11/95

What a joy, love,
What happiness, love,
What wonder, love,
Jesus My Son, love,

Jesus your Lord, love,
Jesus God, love,
Jesus, love the same.

Lord Jesus—9/11/95

On the cross My heart was lifted to the Father in Heaven, and was opened to all mankind as My Sacred Heart.

To help, to give, to love,
This is how to be a follower of Mine.

God the Father—9/12/95

From within your heart look and see with love, for
when you look from your heart, you see clearly what
life is supposed to be.

Forward in love is the only way to go,
Backward in sin is the way to avoid.

To step in love is a step forward,
To step in sin is a step that trips you up.

To run to love is to run to God,
To run to sin is to run to self destruction.

Love...God's gift,
Sin...man's madness.

Lord Jesus—9/12/95

Bringing peace to troubled hearts,
Bringing hope to lost souls,
Bringing truth to distressed children,
I am the peace, the hope, and the truth, found in
the Eucharist.

As I sat and looked out on the people who gathered
to hear My word, I saw all the pain, all the suffering
and all the confusion these children had. Deep inside
them I could see their spirits reaching out for love,
reaching out for hope, reaching out to God. I could
also see how many ignored their spirits' desires and
only thought of their bodys' desires and needs.

What a struggle within so many...so much confusion
and so much turmoil. This state is what makes so
many vulnerable to the evil one's seduction, to his
attacks. How the spirits came alive as My word was
absorbed totally into them, but then how many in their
humanness denied their spirits and put out the fire
that was lit within?

Others allowed their spirits to bask in the word
and grow in God's love. These became My true disciples,
these became My true family, these became the Church
of Jesus, the body of Christ, these became the foundations
of the new life in the body of Jesus on earth.

Lord Jesus—9/12/95

On an altar lies the sacrifice that forgave mankind,
On an altar lies the sacrifice that is often forgotten,
On an altar lies the sacrifice of My body in the
   Sacrament of the most Holy Eucharist,
A Sacrament that should not be forgotten,
A sacrament of love,
A love that forgives all.

Lord Jesus—9/13/95

From within your heart, love all you meet,
From within your heart, love all in need,
From within your heart, love all, for all need love,
   and when you meet them, love them all.

Remember God's glory,
Remember God's love,
Remember God's sacrifice,
And remember Jesus.

To forgive and to forget,
To love and to cherish,
To hope and to find,
All through Jesus in the Sacraments,
All through Jesus in life,
All through Jesus to Heaven.

Forever and ever is our love,
Till the end of time is our friendship,
Always and always will be our togetherness,
One with Me in eternal love that binds us together
   as friends and as family.

God the Father—9/14/95

In truth, all becomes clear,
In truth, all becomes love,
In truth, all becomes joy.
When you speak the truth in love, it clears away any
   wrongs and only brings joy.

Lord Jesus—9/14/95 (Jesus crying at Mass)

To share in My tears, means to share in My heart,
To share in My love, means to share in My pain,
To share in My hope, means to share in My people's
 saving through My gifts,
A share many long to have, but few will accept.

The agony of love, the pain of passion, the torment
 of heart break,
On the cross I had all of these, and I carry them
 with Me until mankind sees its folly and accepts
 My love.

As I looked into the eyes of a young child I saw
 his love, it was pure.
This is the love all should seek to have and to keep.

Our Lady—9/15/95

The blood, the love, the passion, the saving grace
that was showered upon mankind by the blood of my
Son Jesus, when He showed His love throughout His
passion. My Son Jesus longs to help, longs to forgive,
and longs for mankind to accept this.

Lord Jesus—9/15/95

When a Mother shares in her Son's suffering, she feels
 what He feels.
When a Mother watches her Son die, part of her dies.
When a Mother sees her Son resurrected, she is born
 again with Him.

To join in love with Me is to become one in God's
 love.
This is the truth of Communion.

To tell the truth is the way to live,
To live the truth is the way to be.

✝✝✝

Chapter 7.

What Life Really Is

Lord Jesus—9/15/95

Under a tree sat a man thinking of what life really was. He looked back at how he had lived his life, at all the excitement, all the wealth, all his friends and family. He looked back and saw he had always been lonely, even with all he had. He sat and wondered what it was that was missing in his life that made him feel this way.

As he thought, he started to understand that within himself had been an emptiness that wealth, family, and friends could not fill. He started to understand that there must be something more in and to life. What could it be he thought?

Then in a blinding flash it came to him...if this life is so empty, even with everything at our disposal, we must be here for another reason or else we would be fulfilled, satisfied with what we had. What could the reason be? It must be outside this life or else we would achieve it within it. What could it be? If it is outside this life, then there must be another life that we are created for. If that is so we must be here only as a part of our life to come. If that is so it is the life to come that must be sought, that must be prepared for, but how to prepare?

"If I feel so empty now," he thought, "I must be preparing incorrectly, I must be living not in the way that prepares me for life to come. Maybe wealth, excitement, being popular are not the things to seek to prepare myself for the next life, for surely I would be content and at peace if they were."

It became obvious to this man that he had to change and to reassess his values in life. This was a start that would open his spirit to God's love flowing into him, for once you see how worthless things of this world are to you, you start to come closer to God.

All of mankind should follow this man's example and see, are they living in a way that makes them uncomfortable, uneasy, lonely, feeling unloved, feeling lost? In those moments when they are alone and look within to see their true selves and feel that emptiness within, this is the sign to change, to reassess life, and to seek the true life that brings peace and comfort... the true life that is only found through Jesus.

God the Father—9/17/95

To those who follow My word, the rewards are great,
To those who follow their pride, the rewards are few,
To those who turn from God, there are no rewards.

My heart melts when it is offered the prayers of My children,
My heart opens when it is offered the love of My children,
My heart gives when it is asked in love through prayers.

This is the way to save others, love them and pray for them.
This is the way to help others, lead them in love through prayer to Me.
This is the way to forgive others, love them and pray for their forgiveness through My Son Jesus, who is mercy itself.

On a throne in Heaven I sit and watch as My children live their lives. I watch in love and long only to see love. How it hurts Me to see My children misunderstand life, and to be so easily led away from Me. I still watch each one, even when they have turned away. I watch and wait for the moment that they seek My love again, and then I send My merciful love to help them back to Me.

Find within the Sacraments the gifts that are there to help bring you closer to God. It is through the Sacraments you will find the strength to do My work. It is through the Sacraments you can open yourself completely to My love.

Vision after Communion—bright white light became white tunnel. Jesus was at the end with red rays shining from His wounds, the crown of thorns, and His heart. Jesus said, "Enter into My love."

Our Lady—9/18/95

As a child turns to its mother for support and caring, so must men and women turn to their Mother in Heaven. I long to give my support to those in need and I yearn to care for those in distress. My love is waiting here for all my children to lead them to God's eternal joy.

Embrace my Son's love in your heart, and be filled with goodness and joy. Open your heart to my Son's love, and be filled with peace and tranquility. Enclose my Son's love in your spirit, and be filled with the gifts He has for you to share with your brothers and sisters.

My Son waits to fill each heart, each soul, each person with His love so that each can find the true joy of life. My Son waits to fill each heart with goodness and hope so each can reach eternal joy in Heaven. My Son waits to enclose each person into His heart so each can become one in His peace and in His eternal gift of love.

Lord Jesus—9/18/95

United in love, united in joy,
United in eternity, through the Eucharist.

Alone in love, was I on the cross.
Together with the Father and the Spirit, am I in eternity.
In union with all those who seek Me, will I be forever.

Let Me guide your heart,
Let Me lead your soul,
Let Me point your way.

Lord Jesus—9/19/95

To call from your heart is the call I wait for. Many call from their minds, their needs, what it is they want. This is the call from self. What I wait to hear is the call of the heart, which is a call in humility and love.

Throughout time I was, always I am, eternally I will be.

Trust in Me, put your heart into My hands. Put your soul into My heart and put yourself into My love, then trust in Me.

Lord Jesus—9/20/95

Fighting in love means believing in God,
Fighting in truth means trust in God,
Fighting in hope means having faith in God.

Our Lady—9/20/95

Finding the joy of Jesus,
Finding the love of Jesus,
Finding Jesus,
Found in the Eucharist.

Lord Jesus—9/20/95

Into My heart place yourself,
Into My spirit place your needs,
Into My Father's hand place your life.
Find yourself within My heart and see your needs fulfilled by the grace of My spirit and let your life become a gift to the Father.

To treat all alike is a sign of true love,
To treat all differently is a sign of false pride.

Pulling on the heartstrings of love is what you do when you pray. Your prayers join with My love to become a beautiful melody of our oneness.

A man's love is a true treasure,
A man's hopes are a true desire,
A man's trust is a true heart.
When a man hopes in Jesus' love he finds the truth
   that opens his heart and fills his desires with the
   treasure of God's love.

God the Father—9/21/95

   Among those who followed My Son was a woman
who knew how much Jesus loved mankind and wanted
to forgive mankind. This woman had her sins forgiven
by Jesus, and she knew Jesus would forgive anyone
who truly sought forgiveness. This woman scorned and
rejected by many, became a sign that no matter how
much you had sinned, if you truly sought to change
and to love God, that God, through His Son Jesus,
would forgive you.
   How many today see that? How many today want
to change? How many today understand the forgiving
love of God is for all? If you look to Mary of Magdala,
you can see if you change, if you repent and love
God through My Son Jesus, then Heaven can be yours.

   To feel this way, so in love with your Creator, so
in love with God, is how all should feel and then
the world would be at peace.

A step in love is never wrong,
A step in love only brings goodness,
A step in love leads to Heaven.
Always take your steps in love, the love that is Jesus.

To speak in love means to understand the others' feelings
   and not to hurt them.
To speak in love means to open your heart to others.
To speak in love means to speak and act in the way
   of Jesus, for Jesus is love.

God the Father—9/22/95

To sit in peace and quiet and to listen to your heart
   brings you close to Me.
Your thoughts of love that come from deep within,
   should be nurtured and listened to.

Your feelings of joy and hope, that engross your being, should be encouraged and allowed to flow freely through you.

Your prayers only need to be one thought at these times, the thought of love that is My Son Jesus.

From a grain of wheat so much goodness can come. The grain can become flour, and flour becomes so many good foods.

It is the same with the love of God. From one person's love, it can create so much goodness. The love can become compassion and helping others, and from this, others can come into the love of God.

So much goodness can come from one person, just as so much goodness can come from one grain.

Lord Jesus—9/23/95

Do not condemn, understand,
Do not hold in contempt, love,
Do not complain, help.
When you see what is wrong, understand why it is accepted and then, with love, help them to understand the truth.

True love overcomes all difficulties,
True love understands all problems,
True love sees with eyes of compassion that understand how to overcome all confusion.

From within your heart, express your love for God,
From within your heart, show your love of God,
From within your heart, let your faith allow the gifts of God to fill others with God's love and with God's graces.

When a prayer comes from the heart, the words do not matter,
When a prayer comes from the spirit, the words unite in God,
When a prayer comes from the very being, then the person unites in God's love.

God the Father—9/24/95

When a man asked My Son Jesus the way to eternal life in Heaven, the answer was plain and uncomplicated: love your God and love your fellow man. Today the answer remains the same, as it will throughout mankind's existence on earth. Today mankind needs only to look to God in love and to look to each other in love, and Heaven awaits it.

Two simple commands that bring everything to mankind. Two simple commands that, if followed, show mankind the way to live on earth, and how to live life eternal in God's love.

Those in love know nothing else,
Those in love know only happiness and joy,
Those in love know how to give for their love.
In the love of God, know how to give.
In the love of God, know how to bring happiness and joy to others.
In the love of God, know nothing but the joy of helping others and the happiness that comes from bringing God's love to others.

†††

Chapter 8.

Never Deny The Truth

Lord Jesus—9/24/95

The day a Pharisee spat upon Me, I asked him why. He replied, "You blaspheme, You call yourself God, You call yourself the Christ." In truth, I asked him why he did not believe it so, for I had performed many miracles, even bringing the dead to life. I had only ever encouraged My children to love God and each other. I had fulfilled the holy scripture and continued to fulfill it. In a rage the Pharisee beat Me and tore his clothes, and then sent Me to Pontius Pilate to be crucified.

When Pilate asked, "Are You the King of the Jews?" I could not deny it, for I am the King of all nations. After the scourging I would not deny that I am the Son of God, one with the Father, for that is the truth. As I carried My cross and many abused Me, beat Me, hated Me, I could not deny the truth, for the Father had sent Himself in Me, His Son, for this.

As they nailed Me to the cross, I still would not deny the truth of God in His Son, and as they hung Me on high, I never denied the truth, the truth of God's mercy. As I gave My last breath, I called to the Father in love and remained true to His will.

The truth can never be changed, no matter how mankind tries to change it. The truth can never be defeated no matter how evil tries to destroy it. The truth will always be, no matter who believes or denies it.

I am the truth, one with the Father and the Holy Spirit. This is the truth, the only truth as everything comes from this truth.

God the Father—9/25/95

To keep in love, pray,
To keep in joy, pray,
To keep alive, pray.
Prayer fills you with love and joy, then brings life
   to your very soul.

Friend of God, friend of love,
Friend of mercy, those who help.

Lord Jesus—9/25/95

Showering the world with My love,
Showering My children with My mercy,
Showering mankind with forgiveness,
Stand in the shower of merciful love, and be forgiven.

To treat others unkindly is to show your pride,
To treat others harshly is to show your selfishness,
To treat others with love and kindness is to show
   your humility,
Always be humble.

To want to please Me so, is love,
To want to love Me so, is pleasing.

God the Father—9/26/95

Give freely, give always, give in love.
To give freely is to give in love,
So always do this.

Lord Jesus—9/26/95

   The joy you bring My heart when you accept your
failings without excuses, without feeling angry, the joy
you bring to My heart, is the joy of true love.
   Over My heart is a blanket of love, your love. This
blanket softens the pain from those who ignore Me
and do not love Me...the pain which tears My heart
open to flood the world in My mercy.

Love, only love,
Truth, only truth,
Hope, only hope.
I am love, the only love for mankind,
I am truth, the only truth for mankind,
I am hope, the only hope for mankind.

God the Father—9/27/95

Working in love, for love, and of love only brings love...
My love.

Lord Jesus—9/27/95

A way to overcome weariness is to renew yourself in
Me,
A way to overcome being tired is to fill yourself with
Me,
A way to fill yourself with Me is to think of My love
for you.

†††

Chapter 9.

Will You Believe?

God the Father—9/28/95

One day a man came to My Son and asked, "If You are God, prove it." Jesus answered him, "If I prove it, will you believe? How many wonders do I have to perform to convince those of little faith? Even with many wonders, many miracles, some will not believe."

The man said, "I have seen You heal the sick, I have seen You cast out demons, I have seen You raise the dead, I have seen You feed the five thousand. I have seen so many good things, amazing things, that You have done, but I cannot believe You are God, for here You are, a man like I am."

Jesus softly said to him, "You are so full of doubt that no matter what I did you would not believe. You believe, though, in the stories passed down by the prophets and the scribes and yet you have not seen them. Here you see the truth before you, here you see God's love in action, here you see God's mercy shining forth and you do not believe. How strange is your faith! You believe what you have not seen and you doubt what you see!"

The man said, "Give me one more sign that You are God and I shall believe." Jesus replied, I shall give you the greatest sign the world will ever see. I shall give Myself and in three days I shall return."

"When will this happen?" asked the man.

"It will happen the day evil is defeated," said Jesus. The man left confused and doubting. Later when he saw Jesus carrying the cross and then crucified he thought, "A good man, but not God."

Then when he heard of the resurrection he thought of what Jesus had said, "I shall give you Myself and I shall return. The man thought for a while if this could be true, and maybe Jesus was the Son of God.

The doubts returned and he forgot about Jesus even after having been given the sign he had asked for.

Mankind is still like this today. Jesus gives many signs, many wonders, many miracles and yet most do not believe. They say, "Prove to me Jesus is God, prove to me Jesus is real." When the proof is put before them they deny it. When the miracles are proclaimed they ignore them, and when the truth is spoken they refuse to accept it.

When the time comes and Jesus shows God's glory to the world how many will still not believe? How many will turn their backs on God and how many will be lost?

Throw away the doubts, the disbelief. Open your hearts to the truth that is Jesus and be saved.

God the Father—9/28/95

Find peace in My Son's heart,
Find love in My Son's presence,
Find truth in My Son's body.
All found in the Eucharist,
All found in the bread of life,
All found in Jesus.

You have decided to follow Jesus,
You have made the right choice.
You have decided to follow Jesus,
You have made the choice of love.
You have decided to follow Jesus,
You have made the choice that leads to Heaven.

God the Father—9/29/95

To glorify God, you must give yourself,
To glorify God, you must give your love,
To glorify God, you must give your time.
When you give yourself in love by giving your time to others in My Son's name, you glorify God.

There was a man who loved all he met. He helped as many as he could and he gave as much as he could afford. His life was a life of giving, his life was a life of love, his life was a life for God's glory, for he always proclaimed God's love in all he did.

He became a living sign of God in life and a saint in death. All mankind can be like this. All mankind can be living love and eternal saints. The saint is so special to Me and his life so dear to Me, this St. Luke.

St. Luke—9/29/95

The Mother of God, so dear to me,
The Mother of God, so sweet to me,
The Mother of God, so loving for all.

To write the Word of God, you must be filled with the Holy Spirit,
To write the Word of God, you must be filled with love,
To write the Word of God, you must yearn for God's love.

It is a special task to do God's work, to devote your life to God, to give yourself for God.
It is a hard task that never gets easier, it only gets more joyful.
It is a task that brings you to Heaven, if you do your best.

I proclaimed the greatness of God through His Son, Jesus.
I told the world of the Messiah and I showed all who would see, the importance of His Mother.
Do the same now, for the world needs to hear the message more than ever.
Tell the world to take Mary's hand to Jesus, and be saved.

God the Father—9/29/95

A special man, a special love, a special Saint.

Lord Jesus—9/29/95

To love is to hope, and to hope is to love.
When you love you hope for the best for everyone, and when you do this you love everyone.

Hanging alone on the cross, I long for your prayers, your love,
Hanging alone on the cross, I offer you My love and forgiveness,
Hanging alone on the cross, I offer you a glorious eternity in God's love.

Working, working, working,
Loving, loving, loving,
Hoping, hoping, hoping.
Work in love so that your hopes come true.

A prayer of love is your life,
A prayer of joy is your heart,
A prayer of hope is your soul.
Join your prayers with Mine and offer them for mankind.

Lord Jesus—9/30/95

To love means to accept all that is given and no matter what, to give it to those in need.

In love all is possible,
In love all is there,
In love all is given.
I am love and through Me all is possible, and it is all there waiting to be given.

The truth cannot hurt, it is only when you cover it up or try to hide it that it may hurt.

Confusion can be overcome by thinking of Me,
Confusion can be put to rest by loving Me,
Confusion can be defeated by trusting Me.
Think of My love for you and trust in My mercy and then there will be nothing to confuse you.

(Looking at picture of Sacred & Immaculate Hearts)

Mother and Son in a picture as one,
Mother and Son in love as one,
Mother and Son in union become one.
A Mother's love for her Son and a Son's love for His Mother, unite to bring God's love to the world.

God the Father—10/1/95

Through the pain of evil, find the joy of love, for
  when you stand against evil it may be painful at
  first, but then it leads to the joy of My love.

Lord Jesus—10/1/95

To enter My heart, pray,
To be filled with My love, pray,
To become My true servant, pray.
Prayer answers all your needs,
Prayer answers all your desires,
Prayer answers all, for I listen and fulfil your prayers.

In Mother's arms you will find love,
In Mother's heart you will find joy,
In Mother's soul you will find humility.

Put your heart in Mine and become My love,
Put your life in Mine and become My love,
Put yourself in Me and become My love.

Lord Jesus—10/2/95 (Feast of Guardian Angels)

Angels all around keeping you safe and sound,
Angels all around with their love they surround,
Angels all around to keep you on holy ground.

Taking My Body within sets fire to your spirit, for
  when you receive Me, you receive My Holy Spirit,
  Who fills you with His fire and love.

To plant a seed of love within each heart, I placed
  Myself,
To nurture this seed, I gave Myself,
To grow this seed, I give the Sacraments of love.

St. Michael Archangel—10/2/95

Unto the Lord all praise,
Unto the Lord all honor,
Unto the Lord all glory,
Unto the Lord all, for the Lord is all.

To fight in love is the only way to fight, for love
defeats all.

To defeat evil use goodness, to defeat dark use light,
and to defeat sin use truth.

All these are gifts of God given so victory will be
the Lord's...victory in each spirit that chooses the
gifts the Lord offers them.

In Heaven millions upon millions of angels, cherubin
and seraphim, guardian angels and archangels await
to help in the battle against evil.

The angels are the messengers and the ministers of
God's will.

Just ask and they are there to help you and to protect
you.

God's angels, spirits of love,
God's angels, spirits of grace,
God's angels, spirits of peace.

Around your heart place an angel's love,
Around your heart place an angel's peace,
Around your heart place an angel's hope.

An angel who hopes you will come to the peace that
is the love of God.

I hold your heart close to Mine and together we fight
for God. Together we stand against the foe and
together, in the love of Jesus, we will win.

Lord Jesus—10/2/95

A servant of Mine,
A friend of Mine,
A love of Mine,
An angel of God.

A prince of angels,
A protector of men,
A soldier of God,
An angel of love.

An angel of valor,
An angel of Heaven,
An angel of angels,
Michael, My Love's defender.

God the Father—10/3/95

The truth of prayer is that prayer from your heart goes directly to My heart. When your prayers touch My heart they are wrapped in love and returned to you as a grace from God.

The truth of the Sacraments is that they are a grace from God to fill you and strengthen you. They are a gift of God's love.

The truth of the love of God is Jesus, My Son.

Lord Jesus—10/3/95

My Mother looks upon her children and cares for them from her very soul. Each one she loves and each one she wants to bring to Heaven.

Total love means total commitment. A love of God that commits your life to God and commits your love for all.

The wonder of love,
The wonder of truth,
The wonder of God,
Jesus.

On a hill stands the cross of redemption, a hill that all must climb to seek forgiveness.

God the Father—10/4/95

Take My Son within and become one in love, one in spirit, and one in heart.

Our Lady—10/4/95

A love of loves, the love of Jesus,
A peace of peaces, the peace of Jesus,
A truth of truths, the truth of Jesus.
Jesus, the truth, the love, and the peace of God.

God the Father—10/5/95

Try to think of love,
Try to live as love,
Try to become love,
Then you become the spirit you were meant to be,
    and you live the life you were created to have.

Through the pain of sin, I see the love of man.
Through the love of man, I see how sin can be overcome.
Through the heart of Jesus, I see how the pain can
    be lifted and sin overcome.

Clouds gather around the world and cover the light
of the true spirits of God with their shadows. To sweep
away these clouds use prayer, the Sacraments, and
love. Then the shadows will be removed and the light
will be seen.

Under the name of Jesus all is possible, just believe
    and it is so.

Lord Jesus—10/6/95

My love is waiting to fill your heart,
My love is longing to fill your soul,
My love is there to set your spirit on fire.
Open yourself to Me in love through prayer and the
    Sacraments.

To ask in love is to receive in love,
To ask in truth is to receive the truth,
To ask in faith is to receive of faith.
When you ask truthfully and with faith, then the love
    you show is rewarded from My love.

To give freely, with no reward except God's glory, is
    the way to give.

Lord Jesus—10/7/95

Turn to My angels, and they will help,
Turn to My Saints, and they will be there,
Turn to Me, and I will strengthen.

89.

Our Lady—10/7/95

Under the banner of love, life becomes a joy,
Under the banner of love, life becomes what it was
    meant to be,
Under the banner of love, life is worth living.
The banner of love is Jesus, my Son.

A prayer of love, the Rosary,
A prayer of life, the Rosary,
A prayer of hope, the Rosary,
The love of Jesus throughout His life brings hope to
    all.

†††

Chapter 10.

Giving Your Life To God

God the Father—10/8/95

A follower of My Son Jesus, one day gave his life for the love of God. He gave his life to bring glory to God and to show that this life on earth is not as important as the life to come in Heaven.

When they placed him on a cross, as they did with My Son Jesus, in an act of total love and humility, this man asked not to be treated the same as his Lord, for he was not worthy. His cross was turned upside down, and so in death he showed how much he loved and worshipped God.

This man, Peter, totally in love with God; this man, Peter, completely humble; and this man, Peter, another signpost to the way to Heaven; Peter, a true son of God, a true follower of Jesus, and a true servant of the Lord.

St. Peter—10/8/95

Along the road to Heaven you will find many difficulties and many trying times. In these moments do as I did after I was filled with the Holy Spirit, trust in God. Jesus will not let you down, He is there waiting to help and protect you.

Jesus watches and guides your every step and is happy to see you grow so strong in His love. You are certain to make mistakes, for this is human, but do not dwell on them, learn from them and try not to repeat them. If from each mistake you make you learn, then it is not a mistake, but a step in learning to love God. Your path is set, walk it in love, the love of God and let Jesus guide you.

A fount of love was opened on the cross, the love that is the forgiveness of God. All need to drink from this fount to achieve eternal peace and happiness. To drink from this fount means to accept Jesus as Lord and to live as Jesus commanded.

I denied the Lord three times in His hour of need and yet Jesus forgave me. The forgiveness however, was not complete until I forgave myself. How it hurt to think I had turned my back on Jesus not once, but three times.

When the Lord returned to life He showed me His love and forgiveness as He offered me, who had denied Him, the honor of leading His Church. What love this shows, that in His forgiveness He gave me more than I deserved.

It is the same for all of mankind, no matter how much you have sinned, no matter how much you have denied God. Jesus only wants to forgive you, and in His forgiveness, fill you with His love. It is up to each person to accept this forgiveness and accept that he is worthy of God's love.

Lord Jesus—10/8/95

A friend, a servant, a disciple,
A light, a love, a leader,
A hope, a truth, a man. Peter, My apostle.

Standing on truth is standing on firm foundations.
Standing on lies is standing on crumbling foundations.
If you stand in truth, nothing can destroy you.
If you stand in lies, then you destroy yourself.

A family involves loving all in it.
You are part of the family of man, so love all mankind.

God the Father—10/9/95

To trust means to accept what God has planned for you and in that acceptance believe in God's love.

Under the banner of Jesus stand firm,
Under the banner of Jesus show love,
Under the banner of Jesus deny none.

Aroma of love, breath of Jesus,
Taste of love, body of Jesus,
Sweetness of love, blood of Jesus.
Jesus who has the sweetest love to share with all,
  a love that fills the heart with the sweetest perfume.
A love once tasted, always desired.

Lord Jesus—10/9/95

Walking along a path you often look around to enjoy
  the scenery.
It is the same when you walk My path; look around
  and enjoy those who walk it with you.

To feed your soul come to Me,
To nurture your love come to Me,
To grow within your spirit come to Me.
Come to Me and I will feed you with My body, which
  will nurture your spirit and help it to grow in My
  love.

Love, Jesus, different words with the same meaning,
  for Jesus is love.
Hope, Jesus, different words with the same results.
God, Jesus, different words for the same Lord.
Jesus is Lord of love, for Jesus is God and in Jesus
  is the only hope.

God the Father—10/10/95

On the cross, My Son gave His life for the redemption
of mankind. What a gift from God, His own body and
blood given as a sacrifice. When the Lord Jesus took
his last breath, it was a breath that destroyed the
evil one's grasp on souls. It was this breath that said
to the world, you are free of evil, you are free of
torment, you are free to love; you only have to choose
to. This breath exists eternally as the forgiving breath
of God. This breath, the sword that cut through sin
and defeated evil. This breath, more than mankind can
ever understand. This breath, the wind of Jesus' Spirit.

Truth and understanding,
Love and compassion,
Faith and hope, overcome all.

Lord Jesus—10/10/95

Receiving My body is receiving love,
Once you have received, share My love with all,
For it is in the giving that you receive.

God the Father—10/11/95

Follow your heart and find Jesus,
Follow your soul and find Jesus,
Follow your spirit and find Jesus.
Jesus resides in your heart and lifts your soul with
    His Spirit.

Lord Jesus—10/11/95

To fill your heart with love, come to Me,
To fill your heart with joy, turn to Me,
To fill your heart with fire, ask Me.
When you come to Me in love, I give you My joy
    which sets your spirit alight.

If your heart is down, be lifted by My love,
If your heart is sad, be lifted by My joy,
If your heart is unhappy, be lifted by My hope.

I love you and I wait to fill you with My love and
    joy and offer you My hope so that you can find
    eternal happiness.

Two men walking the same path see different scenery
    along the way.
Two men walking the same path find different ways
    to walk it.
Two men walking the same path walk it at different
    paces.
The path is the same, it is only the men who make
    it appear different.
I am the path, but many walk it with their eyes set
    on what they see the path is, not what it truly
    is.

The crown of thorns are a crown of love,
The wounds of the nails are wounds of love,
The piercing of the spear is a heart pierced for love.
Each time you hurt for the love of God, you share
in My love wounds.
Each time you cry for the love of God, you share
in My pierced heart.
Each time you ache for the love of God, you share
in the thorns of My passion.
Share in My love, share in My passion, and share
in My heart.

God the Father—10/12/95

The morning glory shows the beauty of God's love to
the world,
The dawn of the day brings a new gift to the world,
The rising of the sun shines a new light on the world.
Every morning God gives the world the gift of a beautiful
new day and sets His Son above it.

Lord Jesus—10/12/95

Within each spirit is the desire to love God; it is
each spirit's right to love God.
This right is often denied because of the way the spirit
develops. If it develops in love, then it receives what
is its right.
If it develops in sin, it denies itself its right, its
inheritance, its eternal joy.
To develop in love, come to the fount of life, the heart
of love, the Son of God. Come to Me (Jesus), and
develop your spirit into a spirit of love.

Truth knows no defeat, for truth can never be beaten.
Truth knows no shame, for truth can only bring security.
Truth knows no way of hiding, for it is always there
and always comes to be known.
Truth is a gift of God that always wins and always
brings peace to troubled souls.
Truth is a gift that defeats evil just by being.
I am the truth. I am the way, and I am waiting
to stand with each person against evil, and to bring
them My security and love.

Understanding how others feel, their needs, their desires, is difficult, but you must try to do this. Once you understand why they follow a particular path, then you can find the true direction they follow. If they follow in humility and love the path to Heaven, then praise them for their faith. If they follow in pride and jealousy, then guide them in humility and love. By your humility you show your true love of Me, your friend, Jesus.

God the Father—10/13/95

Fish swim together in the sea sharing the same water and the same food. Mankind lives together on the land sharing the same air, but what else do they share? Mankind can look at the fish and see they share and there is enough for all. It is the same for mankind, share and find there is enough for all.

Lord Jesus—10/13/95

Three hearts become one,
Three beings become one,
Three loves become one,
One God, One heart, One Being...God.

Find peace within the Eucharist, the peace that brings
the strength of God into your heart.

A bridge was built across a river so that all could cross to the other side in safety. The bridge did not favor one or another, it welcomed all onto it and saw all to safety. This is how the love of God is; God loves all, regardless of differences. God loves all and offers them the safety of His love, they only have to choose to accept it by stepping into His heart.

Only a foolish man would walk across a river when a bridge is before him. It is the same for mankind. Only the foolish ignore the bridge and wade into the river of sin that covers the world. The bridge of God is Jesus who offers all the safe path to Heaven.

Lord Jesus—10/14/95

Placing your trust in Me brings great rewards, for when you trust in Me I answer your every need, I listen to your every prayer and I unite your every heart beat with Mine.

An open heart is like an open book, there to be looked at and entered into.
My heart is open to all; they only have to look for it and then they can enter it in love for eternity.

To receive Me within is a grace, a grace that should be sought often,
To receive Me within is a gift, a gift of love to share,
To receive Me within is a special joining of our body and soul,
To receive Me often so you can share My love with your brothers and sisters is a graceful gift I give to you so you can give to others.

Love of a Mother, so sweet,
Love of a Mother, so pure,
Love of a Mother, so warm,
A Mother's love knows no boundaries,
A Mother's love knows no end,
A Mother's love knows nothing, but giving.

If you pray, you will live forever,
If not, you will destroy yourself.

If you pray, you will love forever,
If not, you will be sorry in eternity.

If you pray, you will be with God forever,
If not, you will be in hell forever.

Prayer leads to eternal love, when you live with God forever.

97.

To receive a gift, you must accept it and believe in
    it,
To use a gift, you must trust in God and have faith
    in His love,
To understand a gift, is to know how God wishes
    you to use it.

A gift is given in love, a present that fills you with
    joy,
A gift is given in hope, a hope that you will truly
    help others,
A gift is given in trust, the trust I have in you.

In love I give, in love you receive, and in love you
    must share,
In love I offer, in love you accept, and in love you
    must share,
In love I present, in love you take, and in love you
    must share.

My heart opens to fill you with My love,
My heart opens to fill you with Me,
My heart opens to fill you with My grace,
A grace of God's love that fills your very soul,
A grace that opens your heart and a grace that brings
    peace.

Within My heart is a place I keep for each person.
It is there waiting for everyone, they only have to enter
My heart to find their place; a place in eternity.

God the Father—10/15/95 (Feast of St. Theresa of Avila)

A daughter of God,
A bride of Christ,
A woman of love.
A day to celebrate a Saint who did so much for you
    and for all mankind.

St. Theresa of Avila—10/15/95

When, as a child, I thought of God's love, it was as if my heart would burst. As I grew, so grew my love of God and so grew my heart, for when you grow in God your heart grows also.

To find Heaven, follow the path of love that takes you to the Sacraments and in prayer leads you to Jesus.

To find peace, follow the path of hope that takes you to understand how much God gave for you because He loves you.

To find happiness, follow the path of the Spirit that takes you deep into the heart of Jesus and fills you with God's graces.

†††

Chapter 11.

True Meaning Of Holy Scripture

God the Father—10/15/95

Long ago, when My Son came to earth, there were many good people who thought they understood the holy scripture. They believe what they understood to be true, to be just that. Other interpretations were seen as false, only their interpretations were correct. When My Son started to explain the true meaning of scripture, many good people could not accept it, for it went against what they believed.

Many good people denied the true meaning of scripture, because they could not accept they may be wrong. This did not mean they were not good people, it meant they were confused, and in their confusion had erected barriers against anything that may be different. Many intelligent and honest people interpreted holy scripture for others and believed what they said. They truly loved God and wanted to bring God's love to the world.

These same people, however, crucified My Son Jesus, and in their eyes they did no wrong, for they were protecting God's word from blasphemy. These people did not truly understand holy scripture, for if they did, many more would have proclaimed Jesus as Lord.

The people of today are no different. They interpret the holy scripture to their own understanding of it and if anything different is stated, they often do not believe it. This does not mean they are not good people, it just means they are confused and need to be shown the true meaning in the Word.

The Holy Spirit waits to help in this, and if those who read scripture pray to Him for His help in understanding the Word, then He will open their eyes to the truth. Then it is up to them to accept it.

Lord Jesus—10/16/95

In times of trouble most turn to God,
In times of plenty most ignore God.

God's love is everything and everything is God's love.

God the Father—10/17/95

Succumbing to My Spirit, all find peace and love,
Sleeping in My Spirit, all find God,
Slain in the Spirit, all find hope.

Lord Jesus—10/17/95

Friendship accepts mistakes, and forgives,
Friendship accepts the truth, and grows,
Friendship accepts love, and returns it.

I am with you every moment,
Every breath you take, I hear,
Every beat of your heart, I love,
Every second of your life, I treasure.

When joy fills your heart, I am there,
When peace surrounds you, I am there,
When happiness overwhelms you, I am there,
In peaceful joy, I bring you My happiness.

The bread, the wine,
The body, the blood,
The Lord, the Messiah.

As My heart opens to surround My family with My
love, the forgiveness of God's mercy is there for all
to see.
As My heart envelops My family with My love, the
strength of God's love is there for all to share.
As My heart floods My family with My love, the way
to Heaven is there for all to follow.

Our Lady—10/18/95 (St. Luke's Day)

My true son, Luke,
My true family, Luke,
My true friend, Luke.
Luke, of whom so much was asked and all was answered.
Luke, a true follower of my Son, Jesus.
Luke, a light in the dark that still shines so brightly.
All mankind can find the truth of God in the words
of Luke if they only look with an open heart.

Luke stands for love, love of God,
Luke stands for hope, hope in God,
Luke stands for mankind to follow in love and to hope
in the rewards of God's Son, Jesus.

Lord Jesus—10/18/95

Lie in My love,
Lie in My heart,
Lie in My peace,
Lie with Me.

Around My heart, I place your love,
Around My heart, I place your prayers,
Around My heart, I place your trust,
I love your prayers and I love to see your trust in
Me.

ttt

Chapter 12.

Feelings of Unworthiness

God the Father—10/19/95

One day a son of Mine came to Me in prayer. He offered Me all of his life if I would give him all of My gifts. He promised Me all of his love if I would fill him with My love. He offered Me all of his spirit if I wanted it. Of course I accepted what he offered, for it was offered in love from the bottom of his heart. In My acceptance I also answered his prayer, for how could I not when a son loves Me so.

Then he lived his life as if every day was a gift to Me. He lived trying to please Me in everything he did...the joy this brought Me to see such love.

Every day this man had moments of doubt, had moments of wondering if he imagined the wonderful things that happened in his life. He saw each mistake he made as offensive to God, he saw each mistake as a failure in his love of God, he saw each mistake and wondered how he could make so many.

I said to him he was human and he would make mistakes, but if he learnt from them, then they would become steps to holiness. He listened, but found it hard at times to understand this, he found it hard at times not to doubt in his commitment to God. In these moments Satan would be there to magnify these doubts, to increase the feelings of unworthiness, to try to rekindle old desires, and to try to torment with his hate. This man at times felt lost, felt hopelessly at sea amongst great waves of hate and anger. This man, though, always loved God and when he remembered this love, it carried him through the dark times.

God still says to this man, "I love you." God still says to this man, "Trust in Me." God still says to this man, "All will be as I have said." God loves this man and loves to see him overcome the doubts and

103.

feelings of unease placed in front of him by the evil one. God loves this man and says, "My son, your heart is Mine and My heart is yours, unite with Me in love and become My true son." This man is you, and the love is yours.

A love of God is a gift, a gift that can only be truly appreciated when it is accepted in humility.

God the Father—10/20/95

Under the cross of Jesus, find the strength you need,
Under the cross of Jesus, find the peace you need,
Under the cross of Jesus, find your every need.

A mountain stands before you and each step is more difficult than the one before. It is only when you reach the top and feel the joy of overcoming this obstacle that you realize how far you have come. Keep climbing, for the rewards are great, and when you have overcome this mountain, climb the next and receive even more.

Lord Jesus—10/21/95

United, you stand in love,
Divided, you fall into sin.

United as love, you cannot be defeated,
Divided in pride, you are beaten.

United in God, you are a family,
Divided in self, you are strangers.

A cross of love,
A cross of hope,
A cross of truth.
In your life you will find these crosses; it is how you carry them that you show your love of God.

Forgiveness, love, and friendship,
Forgiveness for all who need it,
Love for all those in need, and friendship for all you
meet.

To tell the truth and never deceive always brings rewards.

The words of God touch the hearts of all,
Let all read them,
Let all hear them, and let all benefit from them.

God the Father—10/22/95

Waking to My love is what you do every morning,
Living in My love is what you do every day,
Sleeping with My love is what you do every night.

God the Father—10/22/95

Roses are the flowers of love...become a rose.
Roses have the sweetest perfume...give off the aroma
of love.
Roses show a wonderful beauty...take that beauty to
all.
Become a rose of Heaven, a perfume of love, a beauty
of God's mercy, and show all that they, too, can
be like this.

To join in love with your brothers and sisters, pray
together.
It is in prayer your spirits unite in the love of God.

Lord Jesus—10/22/95

My heart golden and glowing in love,
My heart the glory of God,
My heart given to all who seek it.

God the Father—10/23/95

Entering into a bond of love means giving yourself completely...means loving completely.
Entering into a bond of love means sharing completely and accepting completely.
Entering into a bond of love means forgiving completely and forgetting completely.
Give yourself completely to Me and accept My love completely.
When you accept My love, share it with your brothers and sisters.
In this love find the strength to forgive and forget, for then you show true love.

Lord Jesus—10/23/95

Rescued in love are the souls saved by My Father.
Rescued in hope are the children forgiven by My sacrifice.
Rescued in mercy are the ones filled with My Spirit.

To keep in love, pray,
To keep in grace, pray,
To keep in peace, pray.
Pray, pray, pray, there is no other way.

†††

Chapter 13.

Return To My Son's Love

God the Father—10/24/95 (about Rio de Janeiro)

Away in a land stands a monument to mankind's love of God. It stands as a sign of God's redeeming love for man. It stands and overlooks a city to protect it and watch over it. Unfortunately, most of those in the city ignore this statue of My Son, most ignore it and slip deeper and deeper into sin. Even with My Son before them each day, they sin and sin. Even with My Son's sacrifice in their minds when they see His statue, they sin and sin. When will they come to their senses and return to My Son's love?...When?

Lord Jesus—10/24/95

In the eyes of love all is beautiful,
In the eyes of love all is a joy,
In the eyes of love each moment is eagerly awaited.
In My love each moment of life is a beautiful joy
    that is eagerly awaited.

A true love, a free love, the love of God.
A true love, a free love, your love of God.
A true love, a free love, the love you should have
    for others.

When you meet in love, it is all right to disagree,
    it is all right to correct, and it is all right to be
    corrected.

God the Father—10/25/95

If you are asked, give,
If you are asked, help,
If you are asked, do.
Give your help in the name of Jesus in all you do.

Lord Jesus—10/25/95

The warmth of a summer's day is in My heart when
I look upon your love for Me.

To love completely is a gift,
To be loved completely is a grace,
Accept My gift and receive My grace of love.

Love of a friend, love of a brother, love of your God.
I love you as a friend and as a brother, and I fill
you with the love of God.

Among those who come for help are the ones who
need to help themselves. They come and ask for
healing, and when I offer it they do not accept it,
for they refuse to let go of their fears, their pain,
and their pride. If they accept My love, and with My
love help themselves to become free of their chains,
they will be healed.

Lord Jesus—10/26/95

Love of God in a man,
Love of God in a word,
Love of God in eternity.
Jesus, true God, true man, and true love.

God the Father—10/26/95

Family of love,
Family of joy,
Family of Jesus, the Holy Family.

Family of peace,
Family of hope,
Family of grace, the Holy Family.

Family of God,
Family how mankind should be,
Family to be part of, the Holy Family.

There is a unique spirit within each person and so each spirit responds in different ways to the gifts you have. Some are happy that God has graced you so, and happy to share in those graces. Others see a way of being healed, of having their needs met, their prayers answered. Yet others see a direct line to God through which all can be answered. Then there are those who refuse to believe, for who are you that God should be so merciful to you?

Treat them all the same, love them all the same and help them all the same, regardless. If God loves all regardless, then you must also, for this is true love.

Holy Spirit—10/26/95

Feel My love,
Feel My fire,
Feel My strength.

Feel My faith,
Feel My joy,
Feel My gifts.

Feel My truth,
Feel My light,
Feel My graces.

Feel them within and then share them without.

God the Father—10/27/95

Angels of love surround you to help, to protect, to guide.
Angels of Heaven watch over you to love, to lead, to show the way home.
Angels of God guard you to do My work, to do My bidding, to bring My gifts.

Saints in Heaven pray for you,
Saints of love hope in you,
Saints of God cherish you.

109.

Mother of God loves you,
Mother of God helps you,
Mother of God cares for you.

The Father calls you son,
The Son calls you brother,
The Spirit calls you friend.

So much love for you, believe it, accept it, and allow
  My gifts and graces to you to flow freely to help
  others and to glorify God.

God the Father—10/27/95

Following advice of one sent to advise is wise,
Ignoring this advice is foolish.
Listen and see the love of God which guides and which
  is true.

Lord Jesus—10/28/95

Open heart, open mind, open spirit,
Open to God, open to love, and open the gates of
  Heaven.

Fixing broken hearts,
Mending broken souls,
Filling empty spirits...
The love of Jesus.

Sweetness of love,
Fragrance of joy,
Beauty of Mother.
My sweet Mother loves all, and brings the joy of the
  most beautiful fragrance into the hearts of her children.

The Rosary joins you in prayer with My Mother and
  unites your love in her heart, which is in union
  with My heart.

God the Father—10/29/95

From within, bring forth your love, for when you set
  your love free in the name of Jesus, then all is
  possible.

God the Father—10/29/95

Being one with Me through My Son in the Eucharist, joins you with a bond of love to the Holy Trinity of God. When you are one with Jesus' body and blood, you become one with Jesus' Father, and you become one with Jesus' Spirit. So much awaiting those who accept it, in the body and blood of Jesus.

Under the sun one day sat a man basking in its heat. As he lay there, a shadow came across the sun and blocked the heat. This man could feel a sudden cool change and could see only shadows, not the sun. He realized that once he was away from the sun's heat and light that he was uncomfortable, so he moved to where he once again was in the sun's light.

It is the same for all mankind. Once the light and warmth of God, through His Son, Jesus, is blocked by shadows and darkness, then life becomes cold and uncomfortable. It is when mankind understands what it is missing from the Son, that it will want to return to the light. The movement that is needed to return, is the movement of the heart and soul back into God's love, and then when mankind has come back to the Son, it will never want to leave again.

God the Father—10/30/95

To treat others with respect and with love is the true way to live. If you live treating others as objects to be used, as means to an end, as ways of increasing your wealth, as inferior, then you live a false life that in the end will only bring you sorrow. Live a life of truth and kindness, and live in the happiness of God's love. Live a life of lies and unkindness, and live away from God and receive what you deserve.

Lord Jesus—10/30/95

A man one day was offered two choices. One choice was the choice of riches, wealth, fame, and an easy life. The other choice was the choice of poverty, of a hard life, a life of helping others. This man chose the life of poverty, for he loved God and knew he would have to live a difficult life to serve his Lord. This man is St. Francis, a man who helped so many to love God. St. Francis had hard times, but the harder the moment, the more he showed his love of God, and now you can see the results. To overcome the difficulties that were placed in front of him, he prayed. Do the same and see the results.

God the Father—10/31/95

Pure love in the Eucharist,
True love in the Eucharist,
Love, God's love in the Eucharist.

Lord Jesus—10/31/95

Find My love in the bread of life,
Find your faith through the bread of life,
Find your faith strengthened by My love in the bread of life.

Glory to God, love to His children, and joy to His family.

✝✝✝

Chapter 14.

Trust, In Other Than God, Is False

Lord Jesus—10/31/95

When you place your trust in something, make sure
it is worth trusting.
When you place your life in something, make sure
you give it for the right reason.
When you place your hope in something, make sure
your hopes are not in vain.
When mankind places his trust in anything that is
not of God, then it is a wasted trust.
When mankind places life in anything that is not of
God, then he forgets the reason for his existence
and has no reason to exist.
When mankind places his hopes in anything that is
not of God, then he should hope that God will
be merciful on his final day.

Mother, Queen of Saints—11/1/95

A day of celebrating the glory of God in His saints,
A day to remember the love of the saints for God,
A day to recall the giving of the saints for God.
Heaven celebrates the saints' love and giving, that brought
glory to God.

St. Peter—11/1/95

The body and blood of Jesus today would be a
special gift of love to all the saints in Heaven. When
you offer it, open your heart and send your love wrapped
in Jesus' to all the saints who love you.

113.

St. Joseph—11/1/95

My Son Jesus, a child of love, all of creation bows
    down to this love, this child.
All of Heaven kneels in humility before the Lord and
    thanks Jesus, the Father, and the Holy Spirit for
    God's mercy and grace.

St. Luke—11/1/95

Mary, Mother of God, leads all of Heaven in its
celebration of God's love. The Heavens rejoice in the
love that comes from those on earth, who send their
prayers and love today. It is a celebration that will
warm the hearts of those who ask to be guided by
the saints in Heaven.

St. Paul—11/1/95

Our lives so similar, and yet so different,
Our giving so similar, and yet so unique,
Our love so similar, and yet so individual.
A mystery of God that we are all so similar, and
    yet so different.

St. John—11/1/95

When I wrote God's word, I prayed and prayed. Do
    the same.
When I spoke God's word, I prayed and prayed. Do
    the same.
When I asked for God's help to spread His word, I
    prayed and God answered. Do the same.

St. Mark—11/1/95

The life of Jesus, the life of God,
The love of Jesus, the love of God,
The sacrifice of Jesus, the sacrifice of God.
Jesus, true God, true man, and true love.

When I sat at a table one day with my thoughts on what Jesus had given mankind in His sacrifice, I started to understand how important one soul is to God. If one soul is of so much value to God that He gave His Son for each person, then that said all mankind is equal and worthy of God's love. It is only mankind that refuses to believe and accept this.

St. Theresa (Little Flower)—11/1/95

I offer you a rose of love,
I offer you a rose of hope,
I offer you a rose of grace.
The Lord Jesus in His grace allows His saints to lead
you on the road of hope that leads to God's love.

St. Clare—11/1/95

To rebuild you need firm foundations, find them in
Jesus.
When you build on firm foundations, it will stand forever.
Build in love and see the house grow, the house
that is Jesus' love.

St. Francis—11/1/95

For the Lord, I gave all,
For the Lord, I loved all,
For the Lord, I did all.
Do the same.

St. Theotaxis—11/1/95

Mould yourself in God's love, and then mould others
as the same.

St. Richard—11/1/95

Place the armor of love around your heart, and fear
none,
Place the sword of love in your hands, and defeat
all evil,
Place the crown of God's glory on your soul, and shine
brightly for God.

115.

Lord Jesus—11/1/95

My children,
My friends,
My servants,
My saints,
My love...

The saints—how mankind should be,
The saints—how mankind can be,
The saints—how mankind needs to be.

A call from the heart is always answered,
A cry from the soul always comforted,
A call of love that comes from the soul always opens
My (Jesus') heart.

St. Ignatius—11/1/95

Follow the truth, never deviate from the path, for it
is straight and it is true.
Become a soldier of God's love and fight only with
love, for love overcomes all.

St. Bartholomew—11/1/95

Share in the pain of God's love, for it is by this
sacrifice, you save souls.
Share in the glory of God's love, for it is by this,
you bring glory to God.
Share in the grace of God, for it is by this, you
show others God exists.

St. Jude—11/1/95

Family of God, all mankind,
Love of God, all mankind,
Hope of God, all mankind.
Pray that all mankind accepts its place in God's family
of love, and hope none is lost.

St. Mary Magdala—11/1/95

Forgiveness of sins is a sign of true love,
To stop sinning is a gift of true love,
To repent for your sins is a true grace of love.
Jesus offers forgiveness to all who will try to stop
    sinning and repent for what they have done, a true
    grace of love.

John the Baptist—11/1/95

I proclaimed God's greatness to the world, and I
    proclaimed the coming of God.
I called for repentance and prayer, I called for a change
    in the lives of many.
Most did not listen, for it was too difficult to change.
Most were content as they were.
Can you see any difference today?
The call is the same, repent and pray. The reasons
    are the same, for God's glory and God's love.
The reception is the same, only a few listen. Shake
    them in love, God's love. Bring them to their senses
    and save them from their foolishness.

Lord Jesus—11/1/95

My love is there for you,
My love is there, and it's true,
My love is there for all,
My love is there, just call,
My love is there to make life complete,
My love is there to destroy evil and deceit.

Look within your heart and find Me there.
Look, and see I love and I care.

God the Father—11/2/95

To save a soul, pray,
To release a soul, pray,
To bring joy to a soul, pray.
When you offer your prayers for the souls in purgatory,
    souls can be released from the pain there and saved
    from the torment they have brought upon themselves.
What a joy!

117.

God the Father—11/2/95

Save a soul today, pray.

Our Lady—11/2/95

Trust not in yourself, but trust in God.
See not your weaknesses, but the strength given in
  God's love.
Smile from the heart for God.
Fill it with His love, and it is there for all to see.

God the Father—11/3/95

Enter into the mystery of the universal Lord, Jesus
  the Savior of all.
Enter this mystery by meditating on His sacred life
  and His eternal sacrifice.

In truth feel freedom,
In truth feel joy,
In truth feel happy,
The truth that is Jesus.

Lord Jesus—11/3/95

Taking My hand will help you climb the difficult steps
  that lie before you.
Climb each step in My love, and in My love find the
  strength and stamina to climb the next one.
See each day as a step, and so each day reach out
  and take My hand.

In a family there will be times of disagreement, but
  if you remember you love each other, then they
  can be overcome.

Lord Jesus—11/4/95

In failure find success. From failures learn and correct your mistakes.
Then a failure can become a success.

When things go wrong do not despair, just show you care.
When many problems happen do not be upset, be happy, don't fret.
When there are many concerns do not cry, trust in Me and know I stand by.

God the Father—11/5/95

Love comes from the heart,
Loves grows as it is exposed,
Love becomes stronger as it is shared.

Lord Jesus—11/5/95

Find peace,
Find comfort,
Find joy,
Find hope,
Find love,
Find charity and faith,
Find it all in Me.
When you receive Me within, know I bring all of these with Me.
Find Me and find them.

†††

$Chapter$ 15.

Feelings Of Love

Lord Jesus—11/5/95

Feelings of love are often confused, for evil tries to confuse and destroy love. Love is hated by evil and so it will do all it can to stop and destroy love. It begins with trying to confuse what you feel with thoughts of lust, thoughts of hate, thoughts of jealousy.

See them for what they are, challenges of evil. See them as this, and then stand firm in My love and overcome them. Evil is so obvious, so simple to understand. When you look with eyes of love you know what it is. Now take courage in Me and overcome it.

11/6/95—Vision after Communion of a crown with a red heart underneath, with the words, "Jesus King of Hearts."

Lord Jesus—11/6/95

In the center of My heart is a special place I keep for those who do My work. In the depths of My heart is a special love I have for those who do what I ask. In the very core of My heart are the names of those who love Me and live for Me.

One day sitting by the shore watching the ripples in the water as the fish fed on the insects, a man was thinking of how he was and how he should be. He saw the similarity between himself and the fish. The fish catching insects and creating ripples that spread across the lake, he catching souls and the ripples of love that spread throughout those he had saved and

those around them. He saw also how before he had
been like a shark that devoured all and only wanted
more and how the ripples then were ripples of fear
and ripples of hate. He thanked God for changing him
and prayed he would never return to being a shark.
God had placed His mark of love on this man and
even though this man did not know it, he could never
be taken from God again. This man often thought he
would slip away from God, often felt lost, weak, of
little faith. This man stayed with God throughout his
life and because of that he saved many. Now this
man sits in Heaven and enjoys eternal life with God.
This man, Paul, a saint who was a sinner.

My heart is open to all,
My heart is open for all,
My heart is always open.

A breath of love that opened the doors of Heaven to
mankind.
A breath of forgiveness that opened God's mercy to
all mankind.
A breath of loving forgiveness, the last breath on the
cross.

A lone heart cries in desperation,
A lone heart longs for company,
A lone heart is so sad.
All hearts are lonely unless they know My love.

Lord Jesus—11/7/95

A forward looking heart never forgets the past, but
does not dwell on it.

Love is the answer to all of mankind's problems, for
love overcomes all.

When you walk in My love, you set fire to those
around you. Sometimes it takes a little while for the
spark that is there to become a flame, but it does.
Sometimes it becomes a flame instantly, and then that
soul touches others and sets fire to them. This is
how My love spreads slowly but surely, until one day
the world is overwhelmed by My love

To trust in love, to hope in love, and to live in love is the only way to be, for there is no other way that will bring you to Heaven.

God the Father—11/9/95

A joyful day, a birthday,
A day of gifts, a birthday,
A day of life, a birthday.
A birthday, the day when the gift of life came to be.
A birthday, the day when joy came to the world as a gift of new life.
A birthday, the day that life can start to be a joy and a gift to others.

Lord Jesus—11/10/95

In front of My house is the doorway to Heaven and all who enter will find the way, if only they look.

11/10/95—Vision after Communion of two white doors opening and Jesus calling me to enter. As I did He took me to Mary, His Mother and said, "Pray with My Mother, for she longs to help you."

Lord Jesus—11/11/95

Truth and justice,
Hope and inspiration,
Love and mercy,
All found in Jesus' words in the holy scripture, all found in Jesus.

To find yourself look to Me, for it is in Me you find your true self.

God the Father—11/12/95

Happy to be in My love, shows you have a true love,
Happy to be My child, shows you are part of My family,
Happy to be with Me, shows you love being part of My family of love.

An open door, walk through it,
An open heart, enter into it,
An open love, receive it.
I open the door before you, with a heart full of love.
Enter, and walk in My love, and receive all I have
    for you.

Arising from the grave, Jesus, My Son, showed death
    is not to be frightened of, if you have lived for
    God.
Descending to hell, Satan showed that if you turned
    your back on God, then death held many fears.
The choice is simple...a joyful death in God that brings
    eternal life, or a sorrowful death in sin that brings
    eternal damnation.

11/12/95—Vision at Mass of golden chalice within
tabernacle. Jesus said, "Drink from My cup."

Lord Jesus—11/12/95

Friends share a meal,
Friends share a drink,
Friends share a life.
Share with Me your life, and find your strength in
My body and blood.

God the Father—11/13/95

To open your heart in love to Me brings Me great
joy, for it shows you truly are Mine.

Never forget a friend,
Never forget a companion,
Never forget to love.

Lord Jesus—11/13/95

A little child resides within each person. When this
    child is set free, it frees the spirit to accept My
    love.

Patience, love, and kindness, the virtues needed in life.

The blood of love that dripped from My wounds washed mankind's sins away in My Father's mercy. Mankind needs to accept this merciful forgiveness, accept it and step forward in love to God's glory, the glory that brought forgiveness to all. Mankind needs only to ask, ask with a true heart and an open spirit, then forgiveness is theirs.

When this happens the sickness of sin that ensnares the world will disappear and the beauty of love will bring all alive in God's truth. Each spirit will glow as it was created to...glow with the light and love of God filling it completely. Each spirit will achieve its true destiny, the destiny of everlasting love, the destiny the Father created mankind for...the destiny that is there for all, if only they want it.

ttt